Phylli

Thank you
so much for
your support.

Help us win KY!

Sr Bry

READY FOR HILLARY

The Official, Inside Story of the Campaign before the Campaign

Seth Bringman
Communications Director, Ready for Hillary

Published 2015 by Seth Bringman
Printed in the United States of America

Bringman, Seth, author.
    Ready for Hillary : the official, inside story of the
campaign before the campaign / Seth Bringman.
    pages cm
    ISBN-13: 978-1522765523
    ISBN-10: 1522765522

    1. Clinton, Hillary Rodham. 2. Campaign management--
United States--Case studies. 3. Presidents--United
States--Election--2016. 4. United States--Politics and
government--2009-   I. Title.

    JK2281.B75 2016   324.70973
                         QBI15-600242

Amazon.com ASIN B017AL8QKM

Address inquiries to Seth Bringman, sethbringman@gmail.com.

Cover design by PIVOT (www.thepivot.com) and Giovanni Hashimoto
Cover photos by Kendall Bentsen, Josh Sulier, and grassroots supporters

To four million supporters

"You're the nurse on the second shift, the worker on the line,
the waitress on her feet, the small business owner,
the farmer, the teacher, the miner, the trucker, the soldier,
the veteran, the student, the hard-working men and women who don't always
make the headlines, but have always written America's story."

–Hillary Clinton

Contents

ABOUT READY FOR HILLARY 1

ABOUT THE AUTHOR 2

AUTHOR'S NOTE 3

Part I: Humble Beginnings

READY FOR READY 8

TWO VOLUNTEERS AND A P.O. BOX 9

MY JOURNEY 12

THINGS WE WERE NOT 16

SEEKING SUPERDOM 20

Part II: Unprecedented

DIGITAL EVERYTHING 26

ALL ABOUT THAT LIST 33

BURNING HOT 42

DOING OUR PART 46

Part III: The Players

THE TEAM 54

THE FOUR LEGS 57

THE BELIEVERS 60

THE OBAMAITES 64

THE MEDIA 68

Part IV: The States

IOWA 74

NEW HAMPSHIRE 80

SOUTH CAROLINA 84

NEVADA 87

OHIO 89

Part V: The Grassroots Tour

THE HILLARY BUS 94

MISADVENTURES..98

HAPPY TRAILS 115

Part VI: Reflections

WHO MATTERS 122

READY TO END 133

Part VII: Memories

ABOUT READY FOR HILLARY

Founded in January 2013, Ready for Hillary began with only two volunteers and a P.O. Box. The goal was simple: channel the enthusiasm for a potential Hillary Clinton campaign in every corner of the country and convert it into a movement capable of sending Hillary to the White House in 2016.

That goal was achieved by building an unprecedented grassroots movement with over four million identified supporters and more than 135,000 donors who made over 215,000 separate contributions totaling more than $15 million. Supporters made more than 55,000 contributions of the symbolic amount of $20.16, with 98 percent of all contributions being $100 or less. Ready for Hillary held over 1,300 events in all 50 states, Washington, D.C., Puerto Rico, Guam, and with Democrats Abroad in five different countries. The movement also received the backing of hundreds of elected officials all across the country.

Together, the organization's supporters sent the unmistakable and undeniable message that America is "Ready for Hillary."

ABOUT THE AUTHOR

As Communications Director for the national grassroots movement Ready for Hillary, Seth Bringman traveled to 45 states and met Hillary Clinton supporters from all walks of life. Speaking on behalf of four million Americans who joined the Ready for Hillary movement, he was a major voice in encouraging Hillary to run for President of the United States. A native of Woodville, Ohio (population 2,100), Bringman is a public relations professional and expert in connecting national political efforts to voters in the heartland of America.

He served as Communications Director of the Ohio Democratic Party from 2009 until 2012, playing a central role in efforts to protect Ohioans' collective bargaining rights and efforts to stop voter suppression measures. Bringman holds a Master's degree in political management from The George Washington University and a Bachelor's degree in Diplomacy & Foreign Affairs from Miami University. He resides in Columbus, Ohio.

In his role with Ready for Hillary super PAC, he was interviewed by ABC, Al Jazeera, BBC, Bloomberg, CBS, CNN, MSNBC, NBC, NHK, NPR, and major newspapers across the country and around the world.

AUTHOR'S NOTE

From February 2013 to April 2015, I had the honor of serving as Ready for Hillary's Communications Director. It was my responsibility and privilege in that position to tell the story of Hillary's supporters across the country. This book is a continuation of that work.

The success of the Ready for Hillary movement is both a testament to Hillary's supporters and a testament to the power of grassroots organizing.

A national grassroots movement supporting Hillary Clinton's potential candidacy had taken root long before Ready for Hillary came into the picture, and the organization only had the chance to succeed because Hillary's lifetime of service had inspired legions of Americans to show their support. Geoff Garin, a Clinton campaign pollster in 2008, put it this way: "Ready for Hillary did not create this movement, it channeled the movement, and channeled it in a very constructive way."

A movement was building around kitchen tables, at water coolers and factory lines and on college campuses and senior centers throughout the country. Hillary's grassroots supporters weren't going to be silenced or told to somehow curb their enthusiasm. It wasn't strategic or even possible to ask them to stop talking about 2016. The urgency in their hearts for a Hillary Clinton candidacy could not wait to be expressed.

The founders of Ready for Hillary could have sat back and allowed all of these enthusiastic supporters to act in scattered, individual ways. The staff could have pursued other endeavors and allowed the enthusiasm behind a potential Hillary candidacy to go unharnessed, something that President Obama's organizing icon Jeremy Bird correctly said would have been "organizing malpractice."

Instead, Ready for Hillary took the reins and pushed forward. For Hillary's brand and her political future, and for the sake of her millions of supporters, there was no better course of events. Ready for Hillary allowed millions of supporters to speak in unison with their collective, resounding voices in a way that was helpful to Hillary both before and after she declared her candidacy for president.

As big money threatens to end democracy as we know it, the contributions of everyday Americans still matter. As the Koch Brothers and others pour in millions of dollars, millions of Americans pour in their hearts and souls, and those Americans win. There is still room for the legions of grassroots supporters focused on the common good for the country. In fact, nothing has replaced their collective power.

Despite considerable challenges, Ready for Hillary's supporters planted a flag, organized, survived, and thrived far beyond even the wildest imaginations of its founders. Millions of Hillary supporters joined a national grassroots movement, interjecting themselves into both Hillary's decision-making process and democracy itself. Along the way, Washington insiders mocked them. Media elites dismissed them. Political forces even tried to shut them down. But because of their determination and dedication to Hillary, they prevailed.

Not surprisingly, this book is titled "Ready for Hillary." Simply put, this story needed to be told. It's the story of an unprecedented movement of millions of grassroots supporters encouraging Hillary to run for president. This book is merely one perspective on the Ready for Hillary story, but it's a perspective informed by my unique experience of meeting thousands of Hillary supporters in 45 states. Through my writing, I seek to honor the commitment of these and other supporters in every corner of the country. Their efforts, their energy, and their enthusiasm deserves a place in political history. I hope this book does them justice.

Part I: Humble Beginnings

READY FOR READY

"Is there REALLY?" she said with a huge grin.

During a CNN interview at the end of her tenure as Secretary of State, that was Hillary's reaction upon finding out her supporters had set up an organization encouraging her to run for president in 2016. Her face began to glow, clearly flattered by the existence of such a group.

During those final interviews as Secretary of State, it was understandable that Hillary was more interested in talking about her experience as America's top diplomat and her plans for a little rest and relaxation rather than about her next big step. She wasn't ready to talk about her decision, let alone make that decision.

But her supporters had a different idea. In every corner of the country, in communities large and small, in places near and worlds away from Washington, Americans were Ready for Hillary to run for president in 2016.

They knew she wasn't going to make and announce her decision the next day or the day after that, and they didn't want her to. They knew she deserved a chance to sleep in, read a book, play with her dogs, take a walk with her husband, and do everything else she missed out on while she was restoring America's credibility abroad.

While Hillary wasn't ready to talk about 2016, her supporters were more than Ready to talk about it. In fact, they were Ready to shout from rooftops, "Run, Hillary, run!" and they were Ready to make damned fools of themselves doing it.

They were Ready to do more than just talk. They were Ready to click. Ready to tweet. Ready to sign up. Ready to donate. Ready for a bumper sticker and Ready for a t-shirt. (Unbeknownst to them, they were Ready for a dog collar, too).

Above all, they were Ready to be part of something. They were Ready to be put to work. They were Ready for a movement. They were Ready for Hillary, and they were Ready for Ready for Hillary.

TWO VOLUNTEERS AND A P.O. BOX

A 27-year-old reserve cop and a 61-year-old historian, acquainted with Hillary but certainly never her close friends or confidants, began emailing each other right after President Obama was re-elected.

"What's next?" they asked.

It was seemingly the oddest of pairings: Adam Parkhomenko and Allida Black. Separated by more than a generation, they met a decade earlier at a mutual friend's Halloween party and hung out in the same Northern Virginia activist circles. Neither of them remembers the costumes they wore that evening (I tried to find that out for Patrick Caldwell of *Mother Jones*), but both remember an immediate admiration for one another. They were two exceedingly loyal individuals who loved Hillary more than life itself.

Throughout a decade of friendship, they learned each other's strengths and each other's needs. When Allida had an extra bedroom and Adam was strapped for cash during the 2008 campaign, she housed him in what would later be known to her and her wife Judy Beck as the "Adam Suite." Years later, when Adam needed a trusted grassroots supporter at the helm of an organization that he would initially lead behind the scenes, he offered that important role to his onetime host.

Hillary was stepping down as Secretary of State in early 2013, leaving office as the most admired woman in the world for the 11th year in a row. Millions of Americans wanted her to run for president, and they weren't going to be quiet about it. Her most eager and vocal supporters were not just 2008 diehards; the ranks of her political base now included legions of President Obama's early 2008 supporters. "What can I do right now to make her the next president?" many would ask Adam and Allida.

These conversations across Northern Virginia were anecdotal to be sure, but after enough of them, Adam realized that there needed to be a national organization to channel the energy of Hillary's grassroots supporters. He decided to form such an organization as a grassroots-focused super PAC. Over the course of a few beers on his porch with his now-wife Kirby, he contemplated potential names for the effort. As if naming a baby, they came up with a name for this organization: *Ready for Hillary*.

Just months after their initial emails following President Obama's re-election, Adam and Allida filed paperwork on January 25, 2013 to register Ready for Hillary PAC with the Federal Election Commission. Judy became the group's treasurer.

Adam and Allida's decision to launch the organization was a bold move to say the least. Nothing similar had ever been done before. As I liked to say, no one asked them to do it, but no one asked them not to do it. No big meetings had taken place to make sure all of the key players were on board. No big donors were lined up. And Hillary knew nothing of it. But Adam and Allida, like the woman they so admired, had what reporters Jon Allen and Amie Parnes described as a "bias for action." And they would act in a big way.

"It was our job to lead," Allida said at the time.

Allida was the quintessential activist and optimist. In the early 1980s, she ran an AIDS center in Atlanta – one of the first in the country – at a time when the government and the media were describing AIDS as a "gay plague." She lost nearly every one of her male friends, scrambling to support the Atlanta gay community in whatever way she could as politicians, the media and religious institutions looked the other way.

Adam could have considered more of a political insider to cofound the effort. But teaming up with Allida was symbolic of the cause. Her admiration for Hillary was long held and knew no bounds. In fact, she got to know Hillary Clinton when Hillary Clinton was Hillary Rodham. While she was managing rape crisis programs in the South, one of Allida's mentors told her that she had to get to know this vocal and relentless advocate for women and children. After following Hillary's every move for decades, Allida got a twinkle in her eye each time she said, "I believe Hillary Clinton is the leader of my lifetime." Her admiration and devotion was emblematic of Hillary supporters everywhere. Far from being a seasoned political operative, she was one of Hillary's biggest fans and the perfect co-conspirator.

Adam's lifework, more so than any human being on the planet, has been to elect Hillary Clinton as the President of the United States. The kid is an entrepreneur with a quintessential can-do spirit. If there was an important cause and no one to lead it, Adam would take charge, full steam ahead. As then-*Slate* reporter Dave Weigel described it, Adam's experience included "the failed 2008 campaign, the failed [push for an Obama-Clinton ticket and] his own failed campaign for Virginia delegate in 2009." Yet he was undeterred by previous setbacks, moving on to the next challenge – the same way that Hillary always has done.

At the ripe age of 17, Adam was inspired by Hillary's work in the U.S. Senate on the issue of college affordability. Hillary wasn't running for president at the time, so he did everything he could to try to change that, founding a draft effort to encourage her to run. The year was 2003: He flew to Iowa for a Democratic fundraiser where Hillary was speaking. He could barely afford the flight and walked from the airport to the event venue because he couldn't afford to pay for a cab. He set up shop outside, in the cold, gathering signatures encouraging Hillary to run for president and distributing buttons to other Hillary fans.

Hillary, of course, didn't run in the 2004 election, but her team reached out to Adam and asked him to join her staff. When he got the call, he reported for duty. He put his life and his education on hold. Instead of joining his friends at parties, he checked coats for donors at fundraising receptions. Instead of going to class, he processed checks and maintained a database of Hillary's top supporters. He remained an integral member of Hillaryland through the 2008 campaign.

It was with the backdrop of his initial setbacks – Hillary declining to run for president in 2004, along with her failed bid in 2008 – that Adam decided to found Ready for Hillary. He wanted Hillary to run, unlike 2004, and he wanted her to be in the very best position possible to win, unlike 2008.

Running a multi-million-dollar super PAC was hardly the only thing going on in Adam's life. He was a father. A boyfriend. A reserve officer in the D.C. Metropolitan Police Department. He taught a class. Oh… and he was a full-time student at George Mason University. Even with all these commitments, he also managed to call both our Deputy Director Alissa Ko and I at 10 or 11 PM about every night just to say hi. He nurtured relationships in all of the early primary states and kept numerous players and personalities in Clintonworld happy. He relentlessly checked Twitter and even fed the trolls once in a while. He signed a thank you letter for every contributor of $100 and up.

He must have had more hours in his day than the rest of us.

With the Federal Election Commission paperwork filed and P.O. Box 7705 in McLean, Virginia secured as Ready for Hillary's "address," the organization was official. Two volunteers and a P.O. Box. That's how it all started. Adam and Allida took a leap of faith with the creation of Ready for Hillary, yet the legions of enthusiastic Hillary supporters in every corner of the country made it not a big leap at all.

MY JOURNEY

From my Columbus home, I was watching the CNN interview during which Hillary was asked about her supporters' new organization to encourage her to run. Immediately, I turned to social media to find out if I could track down this group.

Having discovered @ReadyForHillary on Twitter, I tweeted, "Seems like everyone is @ReadyForHillary. Count Ohio in!"

I had no idea who was running this group or what its game plan was. It didn't matter. Whoever these people were, wherever they were tweeting from, and whatever their tactics might be at present or in the future, I was part of their grassroots team because I wanted Hillary to run. The same was true for millions of Americans. No hesitation.

Shortly after my tweet, and seemingly out of the blue, Adam contacted me. I hadn't talked to him since his 2009 race for delegate in Virginia when I gave him a few very small contributions probably totaling $50.00. Knowing Adam's renowned, lifelong determination, my confidence in the group grew exponentially.

We kept in touch over the next couple of weeks and I offered him some advice on communications strategy. And on February 16, 2013, a full three-and-a-half years before the 2016 election, he chatted me up on Facebook. It was the easiest job interview of all time:

2/16, 5:11pm
Adam Julian Parkhomenko
What are you doing now? Pr? Do you work for yourself?

2/16, 5:11pm
Seth Bringman
yep

2/16, 5:12pm
Adam Julian Parkhomenko
nice!

2/16, 5:12pm
Seth Bringman
right now I'm sitting on my ass and tweeting about hillary though haha
so if you need any PR help or an ohio coordinator or anything, let me
know

2/16, 5:14pm
Adam Julian Parkhomenko
Well yes. I have something in mind

2/16, 5:15pm
Seth Bringman
really?
do tell

2/16, 5:18pm
Adam Julian Parkhomenko
I want you to be the ready for Hillary communications director. The only
thing is until we get it off the ground it's sorta pro bono right now. But we
can solidify stuff once we get going full force

2/16, 5:19pm
Seth Bringman
omg that's incredible

2/16, 5:19pm
Adam Julian Parkhomenko
So yes interested?

2/16, 5:19pm
Seth Bringman
i would love to
yes!
definitely. like jumping up and down interested

2/16, 5:20pm
Adam Julian Parkhomenko
Ok great! Then consider it a done deal and Ron Schneider and I will get
on the phone with you in the next day or two to tell you what's going on

We are looking at the end of February / beginning of march for the full launch

2/16, 5:21pm
Seth Bringman
amazing
this is crazy exciting! thanks for thinking of me man

2/16, 5:31pm
Adam Julian Parkhomenko
Yes
This is great! You will be a great addition to the team

2/16, 5:32pm
Seth Bringman
I can't wait!

He went on to tell me that he would only need me part-time, that I could keep my other clients and that I could do the job from Columbus. None of these reassurances proved to be true, of course, but that wasn't important. This was an opportunity to help make Hillary our next president, and I couldn't let anything hold me back.

In fact, not only did I wind up moving back to Washington, I also wound up renting out my Columbus house, shutting down operations of my public relations consulting firm and – this was the biggest sacrifice of all – surrendering my Jack Russell Terrier, Mya, to my mom in Northwest Ohio.

***

When I jumped on board as communications director of Ready for Hillary, I didn't ask for a checklist of insiders who approved of what we were about to do. This was a grassroots effort, and the only 'green light' it needed was from everyday Americans who were already a part of it.

I also didn't ask for a spreadsheet of donors and long-time aides who were on board. I didn't even know when I was going to be paid. It didn't matter. I wanted Hillary to run for president, and I had to do my part to make it so.

And I especially didn't ask if Hillary wanted Ready for Hillary to exist. That seemed to be the silliest of all questions. Why would a potential presidential candidate launch or oversee an organization to urge herself to run? Americans were eager to encourage Hillary to run, whether she wanted that encouragement or not.

A *Yahoo! News* reporter asked me what Ready for Hillary would do if Hillary said she were not running and asked us to stop the organization. The response in her story: "Bringman laughed." Hillary's supporters, I told her, "are very vocal… I'm sure they'd try to get her to change her mind." Of course, in a political sense, if Hillary had actually asked our operation to cease, we would have respected her wishes. But that command, tellingly, never came. Until and unless Hillary told us to shut down, we didn't feel it necessary to second-guess our existence.

To many Washington pundits, the words "Ready for Hillary" were akin to the paperwork a few amateurs filed with the Federal Election Commission. To her supporters in every corner of the country, "Ready for Hillary" was a national grassroots movement of millions. Having lived in Middle America and having traveled the country several times over, it was my job to tell Hillary and the world exactly how much enthusiasm there was for her potential run. That support was exponentially bigger than ourselves, and our organization was a mere tangible symbol of it.

Like me, the millions of everyday Americans following us on Twitter, liking us on Facebook, signing up for incessant emails, taking the pledge, requesting a bumper sticker, giving a small contribution – they jumped at the chance to join Ready for Hillary. This was a movement. Hillary herself could have asked us to close up shop, and we would have, but the momentum around her potential candidacy was unstoppable.

THINGS WE WERE NOT

Because nothing like Ready for Hillary had ever been done before, we had to spend quite a bit of time explaining all of the things that we were *not*. First and foremost, Ready for Hillary was not Hillary Clinton and we were not her campaign. We were an independent group encouraging her to run. This was an especially confusing point for international journalists, who emailed me constantly seeking information or responses on behalf of Hillary herself. I could not resist the urge to email a French reporter the following not-perfectly-grammatically-accurate response:

Bonjour Chrisitine! Je m'excuse, mais nous sommes independents de la Secretaire d'Etat Clinton. Parce que nous sommes independents, les communiques entre notre type d'organisation politique et Hillary Clinton ne sont pas permits. Donc, je suis tres desole, mais je ne peux pas vous aider. Si vous plait, vous pouvez directer votre question directement a l'equipe de Hillary, sa-meme. Merci beaucoup!

But the confusion was not limited to international reporters. A *Washington Times* reporter started asking me some questions about a longtime Hillary fundraiser. I wrote back, "Ready for Hillary is independent from the entities you mentioned and the individual you named is not affiliated with our organization." He quickly replied, "Seth, I must be confused. I thought you were the actual presidential campaign…" And bear in mind this was *before she even had a presidential campaign.*

Local reporters sometimes assumed Hillary would be attending our events. People would send letters or small gifts for Hillary to Ready for Hillary's P.O. Box or headquarters. And best of all, Ready for Hillary supporters would write checks out to "Ready for Hillary" and mail them to the Clinton Foundation's office in Manhattan. It was quite amusing.

***

But while Ready for Hillary was encouraging Hillary to run, it was not merely a draft effort. Draft efforts, like the one urging General Wesley Clark to jump in the 2004 presidential race, are relatively small and typically just a website. Ready for Hillary was a full-scale digital and on-the-ground organizing machine. Draft movements produce little or nothing tangible for a potential candidate's campaign. Ready for Hillary's movement resulted in a massive list of supporters ready to help her win.

***

Ready for Hillary was also not a "shadow campaign" or a "campaign-in-waiting." There was never a guarantee that there would be a campaign, which is why we were encouraging Hillary to run. Further, campaigns-in-waiting are dictated by the candidate-in-waiting, and not only was there no candidate-in-waiting, but we were also independent from the potential candidate.

To that point, we absolutely rejected the notion that Hillary's candidacy was a foregone conclusion. Thus, our primary objective was to encourage her to run by showing her all of the support she had in every corner of the country. Many accounts of her thinking at the time seemed to convey that her candidacy was a done deal and that she was merely toying around with the American electorate. One of Saturday Night Live's cold opens had Kate McKinnon as Hillary, saying definitively that she will absolutely become President of the United States but then qualifying her statement by adding "if I choose to run… I don't know, I'm so iffy on the whole thing!" The real Hillary was truly undecided, and there were serious reasons for her not to run.

One of the all-time best items in the fake-news website "The Onion" was an op-ed from "Hillary Clinton." It read in part:

…when it comes right down to it, I have two choices: Either I spend the next three years of my life investing an enormous amount of time and energy into appealing to the lowest common denominator, or I preserve my dignity, move on with my life, and continue serving the public without completely degrading myself day in and day out…

…Imagine you were, like me, a 65-year-old veteran politician with a sterling record of public service and vast legal, governmental, and legislative expertise… On the one hand, you could put all of that experience to work in the private sector or for an advocacy or nonprofit group whose mission you are passionate about. On the other hand, you could smear makeup all over your face, get your hair done, wear a series of carefully tailored and vetted designer outfits, and try to make millions… think you're likable. What would you do?…

Hillary's decision was not going to be easy. Why would anyone want to run for president? And why would anyone want to *be* president? Hillary had already gone through two presidential campaigns with her husband and ran a prolonged presidential race of her own. There were the Harry and Louise ads, the Gingrich Revolution, the sham investigations, the impeachment of her husband, and the shameful attempts by Republicans to exploit the deaths of Americans in Benghazi for political gain. She also watched as President Obama's opponents disrespected the Office of the Presidency by questioning his citizenship while refusing to work with him to make any bit of progress for the country.

Why the heck would she ever want to do this?

"I've known her for thirty years," Ready for Hillary Senior Advisor Craig T. Smith once told a crowd of supporters gathered in Manchester, New Hampshire's Puritan Backroom, a local Democratic hot spot. "She can tell me 'no.' But I don't think she can tell all of you 'no.'"

Every day, we sought to show Hillary that there were more reasons to run than to not run. We wanted her to come to the conclusion that she couldn't *not* do this. Yes, it was her decision, but we were going to make that decision a little easier. We were going to show her that if she decided to run for president, she'd have a grassroots army of millions of supporters behind her, ready to help her win.

***

Ready for Hillary also did not seek to "clear the field" by scaring off strong, potential Democratic primary opponents. How could we possibly know how the race would play out and what would be best for Hillary in terms of primary competition or lack thereof?

Whether Hillary would run against Vice President Biden, Senator Warren, Senator Sanders, Governor Schweitzer, Governor Patrick, or whomever, the primary election was not going to be easy. The media and the voters of the early primary states were going to make sure it wasn't easy. If Hillary decided to run, she would need to work hard for every vote, regardless of who else decided to run.

Even if it were our intention (it was not), a reserve cop, a historian, and a skinny kid from Woodville were not going to talk a sitting vice president out of running for the nation's highest office if that is what he wanted to do. We did hear some Washington gossip that Vice President Biden's team decided against forming a Leadership PAC that would have assisted Democratic candidates in the 2014 elections because they were concerned such an organization could not match the grassroots support and fundraising of Ready for Hillary. Whether that's true or not hardly mattered because our focus was always Hillary, not other potential candidates.

***

Ready for Hillary was also not banking on or contributing to Hillary's so-called "inevitability." In fact, it was exactly the opposite. Our staff and supporters were working hard every single day because we knew that successful presidential efforts are not built overnight; they are built over time and from the ground up. Not even her candidacy – let alone her nomination or victory – was inevitable; we had to work hard to make it so. If we thought Hillary was inevitable, we could have sat on our hands and watched her waltz into the Oval Office. If anything, the existence of Ready for Hillary showed that we were nervous about the prospect of her not running and nervous that, if she did run, she would be in a weaker position because she had shut down her official political operation for four years while serving as Secretary of State. She was never inevitable in the minds of Ready for Hillary's supporters.

SEEKING SUPERDOM

In a political world increasingly dominated by big money, political insiders and pundit elites, it is more and more difficult for grassroots political movements to break through.

POLITICO ran a March 2013 article under the headline: "Pro-Clinton super PACs – Not so super." I was out with my buddy Rob at Harrison's on Third bar in Columbus and left angrily to share some thoughts with the reporter. The story even implied that the Federal Election Commission could try to shut down Ready for Hillary if it didn't become "super" enough.

Some Washington elites approached the idea of Ready for Hillary with the premise that an organization like ours could not rise to superdom unless some mass of elders was on board. Moreover, they could never get beyond the words "super PAC" in the sense that super PACs could only be big money entities that run negative TV ads, and that there was only supposed to be one super PAC per candidate. "Is this the *blessed* super PAC?" was the question some asked with moderate intellectual laziness.

What some in Washington didn't understand is that our target audience was not Washington. It was America. And to us, Ready for Hillary's classification as a super PAC was just paperwork and the means to organize around a pre-existing grassroots hunger for a Hillary Clinton candidacy. I never used the term "super PAC" when describing Ready for Hillary; the term "super PAC" had a connotation that did not apply to us, because the traditional super PAC model had nothing to do with Ready for Hillary's goals or tactics. The super PAC paperwork we filed was just a legal requirement, not an apt description of the organization. Terry Shumaker, a senior advisor from New Hampshire, also avoided the use of "super PAC," opting for the phrase "grassroots political action committee."

Super PACs were new vehicles for political activity, starting just three years prior following the dreadful *Citizens United* decision. It should have come as no surprise that savvy Americans began using this vehicle in different ways. Yet the audaciousness of one Adam Parkhomenko came as the biggest surprise to many. When Karl Rove, Bill Burton, Tom Steyer, and the Koch Brothers founded super PACs, the chattering class gave those operations quick legitimacy. They were big names, after all. But

Ready for Hillary's legitimacy would come from small names of everyday Hillary supporters across America who were signing up in rapid fashion. It didn't happen overnight, though, and a lot of cynicism and criticism about our organization was expressed both privately and publicly in Washington.

***

It would have been easier to simply ignore the skeptics who questioned our superdom, but to paraphrase Cersei Lannister, when you play the game of super PACs, you win or you die. We played the game and started announcing "endorsements." We never called them endorsements, though, because you can't endorse a candidate who isn't yet running, and the concept of endorsing an organization's existence is a nebulous one. Instead, Ready for Hillary announced that a prominent supporter had joined this grassroots movement and officially encouraged Hillary to run for president.

Fittingly, it was only *after* hundreds of thousands of Americans from all walks of life stepped forward and joined the ranks of Ready for Hillary that headline-making politicians and political insiders started following suit. The Ready for Hillary movement didn't need saving because the staff and supporters behind it were clueless amateurs. In fact, even after prominent Clinton veterans joined our ranks, our staff continued to make big decisions, just with a broader range of people having input on them.

One by one, prominent supporters joined millions of everyday Americans in the Ready for Hillary movement. Big donors, public officials, longtime Clinton aides, longtime Obama aides, and even one-time skeptics lent their support. To impress Washington's superdom-granters, my press shop announced this top-level support with all the bells and whistles of fanfare imaginable. It was a full-court press to meet others' criteria of success in this game. Though, don't get me wrong – the participation of new and longtime prominent Hillary supporters was absolutely critical to raising additional resources and garnering more earned media to make the Ready for Hillary movement even more successful.

So why did these prominent Clinton veterans, big donors, and public officials join Ready for Hillary? One way of looking at it is that they were inspired by Hillary's grassroots supporters and wanted to do whatever they could to support them. Or, the everyday Hillary supporters gave the not-everyday Hillary supporters no other choice but to embrace this movement. Regardless, the credibility of the Ready for Hillary movement both predated and resulted in it gaining prominent supporters, not the other way around.

Of course, others record this history a bit differently.

***

We knew we had achieved a good deal of superdom when the term "Ready for Hillary" became a household name. The phrase was used in headline after headline by the media, even when not referring at all to Ready for Hillary as an organization. "[PERSON X] is Ready for Hillary," "[PERSON X] is NOT Ready for Hillary," "Are [X SLICE OF THE ELECTORATE] Ready for Hillary?," "Will [X STATE] be Ready for Hillary?" I especially liked when the words "Ready for Hillary" appeared in chyrons (words at the bottom of the screen) during cable news programs.

It was pretty incredible to see what our brand had become. Imitation was the highest form of flattery. Ready for Christie, Ready for Warren, and so forth emerged, but none would replace Ready for Hillary in the political lexicon. Best of all was when Republicans started co-opting the phrase for their own purposes. Republican National Committee Chairman Reince Priebus held a press conference in which he announced that the Republican Party is ready for Hillary. Then, music to our ears, Sarah Palin asked "Are you Ready for Hillary?" as she held up a magnet from the Ready for Hillary store during her speech at the "Iowa Freedom Summit." Her comments resulted in nearly $100,000 in grassroots donations for our organization, and we even made her an honorary Co-Chair of our National Finance Council for having played such a critical role in our success.

***

The superdom of Ready for Hillary was due to grassroots Hillary supporters, but it was also due to Adam. He had come a long way since he started encouraging Hillary to run for president a decade prior. The broke kid who walked from the airport to downtown Des Moines was now taking Ubers to meetings with U.S. Senators and millionaires. Back then, he stood outside in the cold during a presidential debate; now, he was running the show. He once sold a just a few buttons, but now he had an entire store of Hillary-themed merchandise. I could not have been more proud. And I'd imagine the same is true for Hillary.

***

There was no particular turning point at which the Ready for Hillary movement achieved Washington superdom, but here are a few key moments:

Craig T. Smith, the "adopted son" of Hillary and President Clinton, joined our ranks. 270 Strategies, founded by top Obama campaign alumni, hopped on board. U.S. Sens. Claire McCaskill and Tim Kaine, early backers of then-candidate Barack Obama in 2008, lent their support. Houston attorneys Amber and Steve Mostyn, along with Esprit founder Susie Tompkins Buell, launched our National Finance Council. George Soros, Laurene Powell Jobs, and Warren Buffet (who didn't even know we were a super PAC) pitched in.

Day after day, we showed that we were super – and it all started with Hillary's everyday super supporters.

Part II: Unprecedented

DIGITAL EVERYTHING

I placed a $50 Facebook ad buy with my own money shortly after I was hired. Adam was gleeful the next morning as a few *hundred* people rapidly liked our page as a result. "This thing kept on going up and up through the whole night!"

This was the first drop in the bucket of what would become millions of dollars of investments in digital advertising efforts to build our list and enhance our organizing capacity.

Digital organizing became key to everything Ready for Hillary did. The latest technology and tools of the Internet made it possible to jumpstart our start-up organization and harness the pre-existing enthusiasm for Hillary's potential run. Millions of supporters were out there, but we needed to devise the best strategies to identify them, and at the lowest costs.

***

Nickie Titus, who had recently been Sen. Tim Kaine's digital director, approached Adam and told him how much value she could bring to the organization. She pointed to the benefits that smart investments in digital organizing could produce in helping Ready for Hillary grow. Adam admired her persistence and used the phrase "she won't leave me alone" at least once or twice. He hadn't intended to bring on a digital director so soon, but Nickie's pitch made him realize that he couldn't afford *not to*. She was an obvious team player, she was in it for the right reasons, and she had a vision of where we could take the organization and how all of the pieces (digital, mail, email, press) would all fit together.

I met with her at a Clarendon coffee shop and we immediately bonded. We shared the same "give up everything for Hillary no matter what the consequences" philosophy. We were each running our own successful political consulting business at the time, but we dropped it all in a heartbeat for this opportunity. Nickie also didn't know how soon she would be paid. It didn't matter.

***

Around the same time Nickie was joining, Chris Massicote and his business partner Eli Kaplan at Rising Tide Interactive also saw the potential for modest, smart investments in digital advertising to really pay off bigtime. Chris was a mutual friend of Adam, Eli, and me, so he decided to introduce us to Eli in early 2013. Nickie had worked closely with Eli on Sen. Kaine's race, and he had her stamp of approval as well.

Eli's optimism throughout our effort was unmatched. He had a great staff behind him, and he was never short of brilliant ideas. He was also never short of crazy ideas, some of which I had to shoot down after long email chains of testosterone ping-pong.

Chris chose Posto on 14th Street in Washington, DC's Logan Circle neighborhood for our meeting spot. He brought Eli and his credit card to that March 1, 2013 dinner. The "Posto Summit," as I narcissistically refer to it, took place before Ready for Hillary had raised even $10,000. We discussed nerdy digital strategies in depth. Eli laid out very ambitious but scientific return-on-investment predictions. We were all in.

Two bottles of wine and a lot of calamari later, we had our marching orders as an organization to accomplish our goals. We were setting out to build a massive list of Hillary supporters, and we were going to use every digital tool at our disposal to accomplish that goal. Ready for Hillary's mission never deviated over the next two years from what was determined that evening.

***

Our initial digital advertising was through Facebook, and through strategic investments by Eli and his team, we expanded our networks to the tune of up to 10,000 new supporters a day. At first, we used Facebook as a measure of how many supporters we had. We called them "Facebook supporters" instead of "Likes." Before long, though, we began looking at Facebook as a mere gateway to additional, more meaningful involvement in the Ready for Hillary movement. Nickie called this the "ladder of engagement," and she had every step of the ladder figured out.

When someone "liked" a photo on Ready for Hillary's Facebook page, it went into that person's feed, and there was an organic impact as thousands more potential supporters learned about Ready for Hillary on Facebook and many of them liked our page themselves. When someone shared a Ready for Hillary photo, it went on their wall and into their feed, increasing exposure for the organization, because that person's friends would be exposed to Ready for Hillary, most likely for the first time. In addition, posts almost always had an action item associated with them, such as taking the pledge to support Hillary or requesting a bumper sticker, so that a friend of a fan could immediately take that action. Ready for Hillary's strategy was to post Hillary photos and posts to have a maximum multiplier effect. Liking our Facebook page was merely the very first action we wanted a supporter to take. We sought to convert Facebook fans into sign-ups at our website as supporters engaged in the next step of their involvement with Ready for Hillary: sign a petition, request a bumper sticker, make a contribution, buy an item from the Ready for Hillary Store, and so on.

***

Photos, photos, photos… Photos of Hillary. Photos of young Hillary. Photos of Bill and Hillary. Photos of Hillary and Chelsea. Photos of Hillary, Bill, and Chelsea. Holiday photos. Pantsuit photos. Hair photos. Hippie photos. White House photos. Swearing-in photos. Because Facebook was such an important gateway for new supporters to join the Ready for Hillary movement, and because Hillary fans gush over photos of her, our modus operandi for Facebook posts was: a photo that included Hillary, a short caption, and an action item below. To many people, it seemed silly, simplistic and repetitive. But it was tried and true. In our infant stages, Adam gushed when we hit one thousand "Likes" for a particular photo. Two years later, we hit 100,000 "Likes" for a post during the Super Bowl using a picture of Hillary as a toddler with the caption "Run #LikeAGirl." It was a play off the debuting Always® commercial in which young girls proudly and confidently run, throw, and fight #LikeAGirl. Supporters, not surprisingly, ate it up.

***

The return on investment, or "cost per acquisition" as the digital folks measured it, was astounding. "We're not even going after the low-hanging fruit," Nickie would say, in reference to our online target audience. "The fruit is everywhere and we're just trying to collect it fast enough."

As predicted, just a small investment in digital advertising paid off big time. We precisely targeted Google ads to likely Hillary supporters, and they signed up in droves. When someone Google-searched "Hillary 2016," "Hillary for President," "Ready for Hillary," "Hillary campaign," etc., an ad for Ready for Hillary's website would pop up. Our web ads were equally effective, using something as simple as a picture of Hillary with a caption such as "Hillary 2016?" with the ad linking to a sign-up page on our website. We even used Spanish-language ads that lead to a sign-up page in Spanish, targeted toward potential supporters whose default browser language is Spanish. Eli and Rising Tide Interactive won a prestigious "Polly" award for that very effective digital campaign.

***

Nickie and Eli had a perfect idea: start giving away free bumper stickers as an incentive for Hillary supporters to sign up at the Ready for Hillary website. This program accomplished four goals: 1) Build our list of supporters. 2) Promote our brand and our website across the country. 3) Build trust with supporters and ensure them that we are a legitimate operation. 4) Raise small-dollar contributions through up-selling. We offered free bumper stickers everywhere: on Facebook, on Twitter, in Google Ads, in emails. You name it. We bribed our supporters and they didn't hesitate, divulging contact information left and right for the opportunity to get something free.

At first, we processed the bumper sticker orders in-house. Our interns Dana, Cassie, Robby, Adolfo, Stephanie, and Joe spent much of their summer in 2013 stuffing envelopes. Staff and volunteers would pitch in as well, trying to keep up with all of the orders that were coming in. Word spread across highways and information superhighways that free Hillary 2016 bumper stickers were now available. We eventually fell weeks behind on the orders because demand was too high, so we started having a mail firm to handle the orders instead. In all, more than 1.2 million individual bumper stickers were sent.

One of the unexpected benefits of our free bumper stickers was what happened immediately as the bumper stickers arrived at supporters' homes. Supporters would be so excited that they'd take pictures of the bumper stickers or selfies of themselves holding them and post those pictures on Facebook, Twitter and Instagram with thank you messages tagging us. It was incredible to see their faces full of Hillary joy – and we reused those pictures to encourage other Hillary supporters to get their bumper stickers as well.

***

The Ready for Hillary Store. This anecdote is amazing: In their book "Game Change," reporters Mark Halperin and John Heilmann recant a tense 2008 campaign conversation between Hillary and her then-finance director in which the candidate expressed dismay over losing the small-dollar race to then-Sen. Obama. Hillary specifically cited then-Sen. Obama's sale of campaign merchandise for low-dollar contributions through an online store. Rather than processing orders in-house and raking in low-dollar contributions, Hillary's 2008 campaign actually outsourced the store, and thus surrendered contributions, to an outside firm. To look at it another way: The campaign gave supporters the option, when visiting Hillary's website, of making a small-dollar contribution to the campaign and getting no item in return, or giving the same amount of money to get a t-shirt, not knowing that their money was going elsewhere.

Adam and Nickie were acutely aware of how this piece should be executed. Very early on, Allida asked her good friend Susie Tompkins Buell to play a major role in the Ready for Hillary Store. Susie was on board and eager to put her talents to use to help Hillary in any way possible.

A close and longtime friend of Hillary's, Susie played a major role in the roll-outs for our store, and she referred us to designer Julie Wertz for our day-to-day design and marketing needs. Julie was interested in politics but had never worked with a single political client until Ready for Hillary. As such, she brought to the table a clear-minded perspective, marketing expertise, and enthusiasm for a new professional challenge. Her time-tested and innovative tactics made our store a big success.

Here are some of the memorable Hillary-themed products that were sold at readyforhillarystore.com: highlighters, cocktail glasses, holiday ornaments, champagne flutes, cocktail napkins, Shamrock shirts, Valentine's Day shirts, LGBTQ pride shirts, gloves, winter hats, baseball caps, baby onesies, car magnets, special bumper stickers, iPhone cases, "Bill for First Laddie" buttons, dog bowls, dog collars, dog leashes, cat bowls, cat collars, blankets, coffee mugs, water bottles… you name it, we had it. We were especially proud to partner with "Rags of Honor," a Chicago-based clothing print shop that exclusively hires homeless veterans, to make a special long-sleeve tee.

The Store also received a whole lot of media attention, and every reporter who entered the office was fascinated by it. "Ready for Hillary Sells Really Creepy Merchandise," read a BuzzFeed headline amidst the roll-out of our store. Free advertising! I especially loved how angry the right-wing trolls became on Twitter when we advertised various store products.

All products were made in America. Always. No exceptions, ever. Ready for Hillary's Senior Advisor Tracy Sefl, who also counted the pro-worker Alliance for American Manufacturing as a client and who had previously dedicated herself to battling union busters, was especially adamant that every store email inform supporters that all products were Made in the USA.

Store sales peaked during the holidays when we had "Order by December 19, Receive by December 24" promotions. In December, 2013, we took a chance on a new product: Ready for Hillary champagne flutes ("bubbles glasses," as Julie marketed them). Within two hours of us pulling the trigger on advertising the latest product, the glasses were sold out. Other holiday items were equally popular. To make sure we shipped everything out on time, we temporarily hired some of our former neighbors – campaign workers who had just finished electing Governor-elect Terry McAuliffe of Virginia – to fulfill store orders. Our executive aide Eric Jeng, always the first to volunteer for additional responsibilities, delivered the thousands of shipments to the post office just in time for Christmas Eve delivery.

The store was so successful that we needed to hire three additional full-time staff members to keep up with the orders. JoAnn Antione, Connor Shaw, and Iran Campana spent day after day processing some of the tens thousands of store orders that came in over the two-year period. By one standard, the store was a complete failure, however: we couldn't design a product that our supporters would not buy!

***

A major project contributing to Ready for Hillary's success was the social organizing tool, a masterpiece of our friends at NGP VAN designed specifically for Ready for Hillary. We launched the social organizing tool simultaneously with the re-launch of our 270 Strategies-designed website.

NGP VAN describes this best:

"As part of the website re-launch, Ready for Hillary is also rolling out implementation of NGP VAN's Social Organizing tool. The ability to connect social networks with our industry leading VAN voter contact and volunteer management tool is a powerful method for targeting core engagers and segment groups. Social Organizing enables supporters to match their Facebook friends to the voter file as they take part in everyday campaign activities like voter ID and persuasion, grassroots fundraising, crowd building, volunteer recruitment, and get-out-the-vote activities — all while earning points and badges to publicly promote their actions. As the only such tool integrated with the VAN used by almost every Democratic campaign and progressive political organization, Social Organizing enhances the voter file clients use for the rest of their field and voter contact work by adding valuable relationship information and other codes to the network."

It was some serious stuff.

ALL ABOUT THAT LIST

Identifying and activating Hillary's supporters was going to be essential to Hillary's chances in 2016 were she to choose to seek the presidency. She had no shortage of supporters, but when she became Secretary of State, she gave up her entire political operation. Four years went by without identifying and engaging her supporters. She technically still had her 2008 campaign email list, but the data became more and more useless each day and each year that had since passed. A plethora of those 2008 supporters had deceased, moved, graduated college and/or changed email addresses. And there were young people in Iowa who were NINE YEARS OLD in 2008 who would be old enough to caucus for Hillary in 2016. We wanted to make sure Hillary had a massive army of supporters, identified and compiled in the most robust, up-to-date database possible, ready to be activated the moment she announced her decision.

***

One of our "win-wins" from the 2014 midterm elections was to swap supporter records with numerous House, Senate and gubernatorial campaigns, as well as state parties.

CNN's Dan Merica reported in September 2014:

Ready for Hillary… [is] exchanging important data about the group's supporters with Senate and House campaigns ahead of the 2014 midterms…

To date, the PAC has exchanged records with campaigns in 14 different states: Six U.S. Senate campaigns, four House races, four gubernatorial campaigns and three Democratic committees and organizations, according to a person familiar with the list swaps.

In return, Ready for Hillary is receiving data from each campaign and growing their list of possible volunteers and donors ahead of 2016…

Barely lifting a finger (Nickie would say otherwise), Ready for Hillary was able to expand our grassroots army of supporters while aiding 2014 midterm efforts by allowing them to reach new supporters and volunteers. We didn't assume every name and email address was that of a Hillary supporter, obviously, as it would have been unwise to do so. Instead, we went with our tested method of offering a free Ready for Hillary bumper sticker to the names and email addresses that had come to us from the various 2014 committees.

***

Ready for Hillary, in a move that put The Drudge Report in an absolute tizzy ("HILLARY MAKES IT OFFICIAL!" was the exasperating and inaccurate headline plastered across the right-wing website's home page in the biggest font size possible), did a one-time rental of Hillary's official 2008 supporter list, paying the fair market value of $136,000 to do so. General Wesley Clark signed an email message to Hillary's list offering a free Ready for Hillary bumper sticker.

But the fact that the email came from the "official" hillaryclinton.com domain name, of course, had reporters contacting me up the wazoo on the day of our staff retreat. This list had been rented by many other political committees and candidates, but our rental was a special case. "LOL" was the response from a veteran reporter when I explained what had prompted the Drudge headline.

Not missing an opportunity, we embraced the Drudge header by pointing out that it was our most successful online fundraising day to date. (After new supporters requested a free bumper sticker, they arrived at a "landing page" on our website offering them the opportunity to donate). The rental brought in thousands of new supporters while also demonstrating to us just how outdated Hillary's official supporter list had become.

"It was really exciting to see you in action," our store marketing consultant Julie Wertz told me, as she was sitting next to me during the retreat. It was indeed an exciting day.

***

Another digital strategy we used was to request a favor from all of our public official supporters who had an active email list themselves. The "ask" was simple: Send an email to your list of supporters and ask them to sign up at readyforhillary.com. We also executed a one-day "organizing bomb" following the 2014 midterm elections. Identical email text, identical tweets and identical Facebook posts went out from each public official who participated, directing the officials' supporters to readyforhillary.com.

***

Our list-building was one-part innovative digital strategy, one-part old school organizing. In addition to all of the digital activity, supporters tabled at Democratic gatherings, Pride festivals, college campuses and the like. We held organizing meetings and info sessions, and supporters organized house parties in every state, while carrying clipboards to farmers markets and other community events. We had kits for everything. Clipboarding kits. Tabling kits. House party kits. Low-dollar fundraising kits.

***

While we did our best to engage supporters in every corner of the country in Ready for Hillary's efforts and assist them from headquarters, but we could not fully harness the support behind Hillary without placing staff around the country. Heading up our organizing staff would be Deputy Director Alissa Ko, who at any given moment played a combination of boss, mother, mediator, and therapist to our team. She came highly recommended from her former Obama campaign colleagues then at 270 Strategies, and we could quickly see why.

Alissa brought on four regional organizing directors who each hired a deputy regional organizing director. Not surprisingly, our Midwestern team (Derek Eadon and Gracie Brandsgard) worked out of Iowa and our Northeast team (Sean Downey and Sara Moe) worked out of New Hampshire. We placed specific emphasis on Iowa and New Hampshire for obvious reasons, but we organized everywhere. Our Southern team (Hans Goff and Kareem Absolu) worked out of our Virginia headquarters and later moved to Florida. Our Western team (Jessica Mejia and Ian Leviste) worked out of California. The regional directors and their deputies were charged with holding organizing meetings, recruiting volunteers, engaging public officials, setting up events and, most importantly, building our list of Hillary supporters in their assigned states.

In addition to regional-based organizing, one of our most successful list-building tactics was constituency-based organizing. The constituency model was strongly advocated by 270 Strategies and it would also be led by Alissa, who happened to be a veteran of President Obama's constituency efforts in Nevada, Virginia, and nationally.

Rachel Schneider, a youth vote guru from President Obama's 2012 re-election campaign, was the first constituency director to be hired. She would be our Young Americans Director and our Jewish Americans Director. Perhaps the most underrated support for Hillary is from young Americans who had worked to elect President Obama and were eager to make history again. Rachel organized college teams across America, establishing them as official student organizations on campuses.

Triple-duty as LGBTQ Americans Director, AAPI Director and Native Americans Director fell on Lisa Changadveja. She is a workhorse whose accomplishments included 3,200 new supporters identified at New York City Pride, 2,700 at San Francisco Pride, and 1,400 at Salt Lake City Pride. The pictures of supporters posing with a cardboard cutout of Hillary were quite entertaining. Hillary Clinton is a cultural icon in the LGBTQ community, and we knew that this constituency would be out in full force.

Christopher Guerrero served as our Latino Director and Veterans for Hillary Director. While the Latino constituency was concentrated in states like Florida and the Southwest, he focused a great deal on organizing in states like Iowa and Ohio with smaller Latino electorates. He also had a deep grasp of the diversity within the Latino community. Hillary's strong performance among Latino voters in the 2008 primary was a particular area of support that we knew we could harness going into 2016.

Black Americans and faith community supporters were organized by Quentin James, who brought early Obama credentials and early state South Carolina roots to the table. The black community was and is strongly in the Clintons' corner, despite narratives to the contrary. Hillary's biggest demographic weakness in 2008 is now arguably her biggest demographic strength. Former Atlanta mayor Shirley Franklin became a senior advisor, helping organize and to tell the story of the community's strong support.

Last but not least of our constituency directors was Jessica Grounds, who served as Director of the Ready for Hillary Women's Office and hired China Dickerson as her Deputy Director. They organized women through house parties, fundraising events, and peer-to-peer programs. The prospect of electing the first woman president was not surprisingly a major motivation and communication tactic in outreach toward women. As Hillary once said, "If we can blast 50 women into space, we will someday launch a woman into the White House."

***

In addition to building a massive list of supporters, we had to make sure that every detail on that list was entered, usable, "de-duped," accurate, integrated, and so forth. Did I mention "usable?" Our long-term mission would be undermined if other campaign operatives (ie, ones that would be hired on a campaign that did not yet exist!) couldn't use our data. I won't pretend to know the intricacies of how data works. That task fell on Ready for Hillary Data Director Amy Drummond and Deputy Data Director Jane Miller, and they were great at it. Here's an anecdote: Amy and Jane would rectify inaccurate email addresses. So, if a supporter signed up by entering @gamil or @gmial instead of @gmail, or if a volunteer made a similar data entry error, Amy and Jane would go through and make sure to correct the error so that we would have a usable email address. In addition, with the hundreds of thousands of handwritten sign-ups coming in from events across the country, they had to make sure the data was entered in a timely manner so that we could quickly engage the new supporters in our movement. Amy and Jane trained data entry volunteers at our headquarters and held online trainings with volunteers across the country to manage this big task.

***

It took a tremendous amount of resources to build our list. Matt Felan, Hillary's deputy finance director in 2008, was brought on early as Ready for Hillary's Finance Director and helped to bring big donors on board. A lot was riding on our first Federal Election Commission report that was to be filed on July 31, 2013. It was a make-or-break opportunity to show that our organization was serious. Craig, Adam, Matt, and Allida worked the phones nonstop, enabling us to exceed our seven-figure goal and raise $1.25 million for the first filing period. We had planted the flag and showed we could raise the resources necessary to be successful. By the end of 2013, we had surpassed $4 million. In total, 135,000 Americans owned a piece of the Ready for Hillary movement, with 98 percent of contributions being in the amount of $100 or less.

The daily, heavy lifting of the large-dollar fundraising efforts fell on Deputy Finance Director Alex Smith. Alex, who came to us by way of Dewey Square Group, was responsible for recruiting and engaging our finance council, which grew to 900 donors. Finance Council members pledged to write or raise $5,000, while Finance Council co-chairs pledged to raise $25,000. Alex helped the finance council members meet their individual goals. She and Grassroots Fundraising Director Neisha Blandin also launched a Millennial Council fundraising arm, chaired by former South Carolina State Rep. Bakari Sellers and Missouri Secretary of State and now-U.S. Senate candidate Jason Kander. Adam did a tremendous amount of donor calls and meetings to help us make payroll while continuing our aggressive digital advertising efforts. In the latter months of Ready for Hillary's existence, he even hired finance staffer Andrew Simpson to keep himself on track.

Mary Pat Bonner and Allison Thompson at the Bonner Group, along with Rafi Jafri in New York, were clutch players who helped us raise the larger contributions and meet our fundraising goals. Across the country, we set up high-dollar receptions that often featured Craig, former Michigan governor Jennifer Granholm, or another big name as a surrogate speaker to help draw a crowd. Even our Americans Abroad supporters got in on the fun, and Allida would either make an international trip to headline their events or join them via Skype.

***

In early summer 2013, my former intern Krista Collard, then living in San Francisco and working for the Sierra Club, started proposing ways that she could activate her network of women in the Bay Area to help grow the Ready for Hillary movement. That network of young professional women, appropriately named "Women Get It Done," also included Kate Maeder, Rachel Huennekens, Shilpa Grover, Niki Hinton, and Kimberly Ellis. This group of dynamic women definitely got it done.

A week before the event, Craig was in San Francisco holding a series of meetings with big donors. After one meeting, he called Adam. "Hey did you know that there's a group of women organizing a low-dollar fundraiser for us in San Francisco?"

"Yes, Craig. Seth has been talking to them every day," was Adam's nonchalant response.

Craig paused, then added, "We should do one of those every week!"

Thus began a series of $20.16 fundraisers across the country.

"We have no staff to help you and we can't fly anyone out to speak," I warned the Bay Area women, urging them to hold off for a month or two when we would be able to support them more. It didn't matter to them; they were marching forward with the event, which took place at the Women's Building in San Francisco's Mission District. Scrambling and disorganized, our then-tiny staff secured Clinton White House alum Chris Lavery as the speaker just hours before the event. 120 women and a handful of men attended, each giving $20.16. It was a tremendous success and a demonstration of the commitment of Hillary's supporters.

Not to be outdone by their Northern California counterparts, a group of supporters in SoCal led by Ready for Hillary Senior Advisor Michael Trujillo and my longtime karaoke partner Catherine Landers began organizing their own event in Los Angeles. The event was complete with valet parking, red carpet, a photo booth, and even an appearance from reality TV star Omarosa Manigault-Stallworth. The *Washington Post*'s Matea Gold reported from the scene, "Inside the L.A. club Wednesday night, more than 400 mostly twentysomething fans of Hillary Rodham Clinton milled around the cavernous dance floor, sipping $8 drinks such as The Rodham (Jack Daniels with peach schnapps, sweet & sour, orange juice, 7-Up and a splash of grenadine) as local politicos exhorted them to prepare for another Clinton presidential run."

Following those news reports, supporters across the country came out of the woodwork and began organizing their own $20.16 events with local flare, "Cardboard Hillary," and *approved* Hillary-themed cocktails. ("The Ceiling Breaker" was often on the menu, while "The Foggy Bottom" was nixed from an LGBTQ event… blame Lisa). Junelle Cavero Harnal, an alum of Hillary's 2008 campaign living in Arizona, began organizing events in Phoenix, Flagstaff and Tucson. With such a level of enthusiasm, it became obvious that Ready for Hillary needed a staff member dedicated to helping supporters execute local grassroots fundraising events. Neisha, a veteran fundraiser in New York and New Jersey, was selected for the role.

The routine grassroots fundraisers across the country became emblematic of the Ready for Hillary movement. Functionally, the events were as much about raising money as they were about showcasing support for Hillary. Neisha and I were always on the same page with our event organizers: reserve a small room and pack it with bodies, open the event to the media, and take lots of pictures for Facebook and Twitter.

Hundreds of young professionals packing into the same room, each monetarily invested in Hillary's potential candidacy, was exactly what we wanted the media to witness. No other potential candidate summoned this amount of early excitement, investment, and action. "I've seen everything I need to see here," one New York-based reporter told me toward the beginning of a 300-plus person event atop The Standard hotel. "I can barely breathe in this place. I'm going to head out." I just stood there and smiled, thanking him for stopping by.

Just as inspiring as the size of the crowds was the diversity among them. "We are a mosaic of America tonight," former State Senator Nina Turner told two hundred elected officials, Labor leaders and activists gathered at Market Garden Brewery in Cleveland on a snowy February 2015 evening.

Because of these events, high-ranking Democratic supporters began lining up behind Hillary and headlining Ready for Hillary events for the most grassroots of all reasons: because local activists asked them to do so. In 2008, Hillary's campaign spent a great deal of time and effort securing endorsements, but in many states Democratic activists largely ignored their public officials' recommendation. Going into 2016, however, Democratic activists were approaching their public officials and urging them to support Hillary. It was a complete turnaround.

With success came more success. Mayors, Members of Congress, U.S. Senators and others were headlining events in their states. "I'm only doing a high-dollar event if you have a low-dollar event here as well," one big-city mayor told us when our finance staff reached out requesting his presence at a high-dollar event. We were quick to oblige.

100 supporters in Buffalo. 100 in Columbus, twice. 100 in Columbia. 100 in Towson, Maryland. 150 in Pittsburgh. 150 in Seattle. 150 in Richmond. 200 in Cleveland. 200 in Jacksonville. 200 in Boston. 300 in Philadelphia. 300 in New York. 200, 300, and 400 in Washington. 300 and 400 in Los Angeles. And the largest event of all: 600(!) supporters in Hillary's early stomping grounds of Chicago, joining Sen. Dick Durbin and an array of other high-ranking officials, all perfectly on message.

By the end of the Ready for Hillary effort, what started with a handful of young professional women in the Bay Area resulted in a list of more than 55,000 Americans all making a contribution in the amount of exactly $20.16.

***

In the end, and thanks to the efforts of four supporters, Ready for Hillary built a list of four million identified supporters. 135,000 financial contributors owned a piece of the Ready for Hillary movement, and their names and contact information were all perfectly preserved and easily exchanged. Hillary started began her 2016 campaign with a larger supporter list than she had at the end of her 2008 campaign. It was, as POLITICO's Annie Karni called it, "a data gold mine that will immediately bolster the Democratic front-runner's fundraising and organizing efforts." Annie also provided a key anecdote from observing a Hillary for America organizer in Nevada who attempted to use Hillary's 2008 list to recruit volunteers: many of those past volunteers were deceased.

The mission and work of Ready for Hillary's supporters was validated. Mission Accomplished.

BURNING HOT

Adam reached out for advice from one prominent Clintonista right around the time he was filing the paperwork to establish Ready for Hillary as a super political action committee. He gave Adam some sound advice: "First piece of advice: Get a good lawyer. Second piece of advice: Get a good lawyer."

Indeed, we would get a good lawyer: Jim Lamb of Sandler, Reiff, Young and Lamb.

Jim – like Craig and many other "adults" in our operation – was so enthusiastic about what we were doing at Ready for Hillary. He was almost like a kid in a candy store. He'd spend a day or two at our headquarters here and there to get away from his office. Clearly, none of his clients were as fun as us.

Adam thought that the fact that we hired Jim was newsworthy. I was skeptical of course; everyone in town has a lawyer. But I gave Cameron Joseph from *The Hill* a call. Cameron was the first to report on the creation of Ready for Hillary, having seen our Statement of Organization on the Federal Elections Committee website.

Cameron's story went up within an hour. Five minutes after the story posted, I got a call from CNN.

"Can you confirm The Hill's story," the CNN reporter asked, "even on background?"

"Umm. Yes," I responded.

"Okay great. Keep us in mind anytime you have an exclusive like this in the future."

"Absolutely," I said, while thinking, "WTF dude, you're CNN. Why do you care about this?"

Such was the media fascination with Hillary Clinton. The word "Hillary" in anyone's headline was click-gold. Every sentence she uttered was a headline. Every time she appeared in public and *didn't declare her candidacy*, well, that was a headline, too. If she weighed in on any topic, headline. If she didn't weigh in on any topic, also headline.

Because the media was so focused on Hillary, they were also extremely focused on everything Ready for Hillary did. In a previous role as Ohio Democratic Party Communications Director, working with reporters in mostly-vacant newsrooms, it was like pulling teeth to get reporters to write stories. I'd get my hopes up, call a reporter, and then get that sinking feeling in my stomach like someone attractive just gave me the cold shoulder at a bar. This job meant no more cold shoulders for me. The proverbial hotties were lining up and throwing themselves on me now. They were even furious at times when I didn't ask them out. (For the record, I did circle back with that CNN reporter and give him the exclusive when we made our next big hire, Matt Felan as Finance Director).

Media outlets have entire groups of reporters dedicated to covering her. CNN has nearly enough to field a baseball team. The *New York Times* started a trend in 2013 of assigning and announcing with fanfare an exclusive Hillary-focused reporter. This was an unprecedented amount of attention devoted to a non-candidate so early in the presidential cycle, and it meant a whole lot of media inquiries at Ready for Hillary. POLITICO won the award for most reporters to contact Ready for Hillary (around 15), with Bloomberg a close second. Compare that to the local newspapers back home shutting down bureaus and buying out lifelong journalists rather than paying the costs of having them complete their careers…

As I sat in my 5th floor office of our Rosslyn headquarters typing a press release, I would glance over at Washington and laugh, yelling out to the team across the hall: "We're causing earthquakes!! Earthquake begins in 30 minutes, folks!!" We knew when we were about to make big news.

The first earthquake we caused was courtesy of James Carville.

Aaron Blake of the *Washington Post* got a scoop that James Carville signed an email that would go out to all Ready for Hillary supporters. Carville's message was a masterpiece crafted by Eli, and it read in part:

"I'm not going to waste my time writing you about how great Hillary is or how formidable she'd be – you know it all already. But it isn't worth squat to have the fastest car at the racetrack if there ain't any gas in the tank -- and that's why the work that Ready for Hillary PAC is doing is absolutely critical. We need to convert the hunger that's out there for Hillary's candidacy into a real grassroots organization."

All very true! The *Post* story went up online at exactly 7:00 a.m. It was good stuff. I read it and fell back asleep at 7:04, but then my phone rang at 7:06. The phone didn't stop ringing.

I then received an only-somewhat-friendly email from one of the more prominent Hillary-focused reporters out there, telling me in no uncertain terms that a heads up would be appreciated the next time we make a big announcement.

Carville was taken aback, as were we, by the amount of media attention his email received, given that he signs emails for all kinds of organizations, few in which he is intimately involved. Aaron's article was accurate, but the story took on a life of its own as various media reports exaggerated his involvement in our then-new organization, with some saying that he had become an official advisor. The Ragin' Cajun was a guest on a HuffPost Live segment the next day, clearing things up by saying, "I SIGNED AN EEEEMAIL!!! MAYBE I SIGN TOO MANY EEMAILS!!!" Avery Jaffe, my then-intern and a very talented vocal impersonator, mimicked that line often.

***

In the months that followed, I was determined to continue to make as much of an earned media splash as possible with each new development in the growth of our organization. We had the opportunity to get our name out there, and unless I heard otherwise I was going to maximize every earned media opportunity. After months of intense coverage, I received what I referred to as a "directive from above."

"We're burning too hot," Craig would say. "I've been fixin' to tell ya," he prefaced his warning, in colloquial Arkansan.

When I started with Ready for Hillary in late February 2013, we issued a press release nearly every day on whatever came to mind, if for nothing else just to remind everyone that we existed. A year later, we were sending about one press release a month as we focused on our organizing work.

Some people thought Ready for Hillary was turning Hillary into more of a political figure. It was a reasonable argument that we simply did not buy. She was going to be thought of as a political figure regardless of Ready for Hillary's existence. She was going to be covered as a potential presidential candidate whether we were organizing her supporters or not. But as Craig correctly made clear, we could afford to dial things down a notch, and we did.

***

"Nothing like this has ever been done before," we often said. One reporter gave me grief over how many times I used the word "unprecedented." Being unprecedented brought about unprecedentedly challenging questions, however, and sometimes Ready for Hillary just didn't have the answers quite yet.

What happens if she doesn't run? How would the list be transferred? What would happen to Ready for Hillary if and when she announces? No similar questions had been confronted by another organization before, and we certainly didn't have definitive answers for them right away. There was no blueprint for any of what we were doing, so we had to figure it out along the way. Supporters, advisors, staff or consultants came up with innovative ideas and we would adjust our tactics accordingly. But our basic mission never changed. "We're continuing to build the list," was my go-to answer whenever any topic that I didn't want to address came up. Our staff was often counseled to begin sentences with the words, "Right now, our focus is…" and end sentences with "…all the rest will come later."

DOING OUR PART

In addition to navigating the legal and logistical waters in this unprecedented venture, we sought to be nimble and adapt wherever possible to achieve our overarching goals and support important causes that came long before the 2016 campaign.

When Hillary gave a sweeping speech on voting rights before the American Bar Association, our digital team had a great idea: We should send out an email to our list and post on social media asking supporters to sign a petition to stand with Hillary on voting rights. Specifically, we asked supporters to join Hillary in calling on Congress to fix the Voting Rights Act – a problem created by the Supreme Court in a 5-4 party-line decision that immediately led to a fury of voter disenfranchisement moves against black voters in the South. The petition strategy helped build our list and it told us more about individual supporters and what motivates them.

Particularly important, I believe, were our efforts to harness the enthusiasm for Hillary to help advocate President Obama's agenda. As soon as Hillary added her voice to an Obama Administration priority, we got the wheels turning and urged our supporters to add their voices as well. The goal was to give Hillary more political firepower in the absence of her having a political operation and active email list. For instance, we encouraged our supporters who were uninsured to go to healthcare.gov and sign up for health coverage – or to encourage any of their uninsured friends to do so. The email was appropriately signed by Mark Alexander, a policy advisor to President Obama during the push for Obamacare. This approach was a win for us, a win for Hillary, an opportunity for our supporters, and a way for us to show that we were mobilizing our grassroots army for more than just electing Hillary Clinton; we were seeking to help the Democratic Party as a whole. It was the least we could do.

***

One day, I came in to the office and suddenly found out that Ready for Hillary had just become something called a "hybrid PAC." How did I learn this information? In a tweet from Dave Levinthal of the Center for Public Integrity. Then, I hopped on Google to try to find out what the heck a hybrid PAC was.

I called Adam right away. "You're telling me that Amy just changed our entire status as an organization under the Federal Elections Commission and she didn't bother to tell me?" I guess both Amy and Adam thought that the other had briefed me on what was about to occur.

I then called Amy. Amy Wills Gray was our one-of-a-kind Operations Director who worked from her home in Michigan. I loved every time we interacted, and I couldn't get mad at her, even at a time like this. "Okay, Amy. Hybrid PAC. Tell me what you just did." She let out a big laugh and walked me through it, then I returned the calls from the sixteen or so reporters who had contacted us in the meantime.

With Jim walking us through every step, Ready for Hillary became both a super PAC (operating and using resources independently from any candidate or candidate committee) and a traditional PAC (coordinating directly with candidates or candidate committees, with the ability to make direct contributions to candidates). We maintained separate bank account for each of the two components of the hybrid.

Hillary didn't have a leadership PAC – a standard mechanism to dole out checks to candidates in early primary states and build political goodwill leading up to a probable presidential candidacy. But Ready for Hillary could raise money into a separate account operating as a traditional political action committee, and use those funds to help 2014 candidates Hillary supported. We did our part by cutting checks to candidates and state parties in early states and across the country. All told, Ready for Hillary devoted about $500,000 in direct donations toward efforts to elect Democrats in 2014.

***

Another major part of our 2014 commitment was the deployment of nearly our entire staff. We emptied our offices and hit the road to help Democratic efforts in early primary and caucus states, as well as in key U.S. Senate races.

Lisa was the first to deploy, taking an official position as GOTV Director for the U.S. Senate race in Colorado. Rachel and Eric joined Derek and Gracie in Iowa. Nickie, Evan Wessel and Sam Levison focused their efforts on New Hampshire with Sean Downey and Sara. Hans, Kareem and China went to South Carolina. Jess Mejia, Ian and Amy Drummond (along with her dog Lila, who stayed at "Camp Bow Wow" – a vendor listed on our Federal Election Commission report, no kidding) to Nevada. Connor embarked for Alaska (because, why not?) and Allida, Arkansas. Gabi Kahn headed to Kentucky, Quentin to Ohio, Sean England to Louisiana, Christopher to Maine, Neisha to Minnesota, JoAnn to Michigan, and Jessica Grounds to North Carolina. Each staffer gained valuable experience, met Hillary supporters in the states, and helped build that all-important goodwill with Democrats across the country.

Iran organized a group of about 20 volunteers who took off from Washington to New Hampshire for GOTV weekend. I scurried around the country with Kendall Bentsen, my unofficial co-pilot.

***

While our staff was on the road, Ready for Hillary engaged supporters across the country, aiming to do everything we could to channel the enthusiasm around a potential Hillary candidacy into helping elect Democrats up and down the ballot.

First and foremost, through digital, social media and on-the-ground efforts, we asked every supporter to pledge to vote for Democrats in 2014. When signing up new supporters at events throughout the country, we set aside the normal Ready for Hillary sign-up sheets and used "Ready to Vote" cards that included information on the importance of the 2014 midterm elections.

Next, we sent emails to our list asking every one of our supporters to sign up to volunteer to help Democrats in 2014, and we connected those supporters to local Democratic state parties or campaigns. We asked our supporters to "work as hard in the 2014 midterms as we would if Hillary were on the ballot, because it's that important." Our website also allowed supporters to look up their polling place and, no matter where they lived, to make calls on Ready for Hillary's user-friendly National Call Tool and reach voters in key 2014 states. In addition to asking our supporters to vote and volunteer, Ready for Hillary halted our own low-dollar fundraising efforts and encouraged supporters to make direct financial contributions to candidates who Hillary supported.

Everything was like clockwork. Once Hillary announced a campaign event for a particular candidate, Ready for Hillary delivered a digital support package of sorts to that candidate. We immediately spread the word of Hillary's campaign appearances and invited our local supporters to attend. After the rally, we took quotes from Hillary's stump speeches, in which she talked about why she supports that candidate, and we incorporated those quotes into fundraising pitches in which we asked supporters nationwide to join Hillary in supporting those candidates. Then, we asked supporters to volunteer directly for those candidates.

Molly Crosby and Eli over at Rising Tide Interactive were on the ball, quickly churning out these emails. Evan and Nickie were doing double duty from New Hampshire, keeping our digital and social efforts rolling across the country while working on the ground to help Granite State Democrats. And on several occasions I had to pull over the Hillary Bus to the side of the road to quickly proofread an email before it was blasted out to supporters. Those were some ridiculously fun times.

***

Meanwhile, on the Hillary Bus, we chased Hillary around the country, bookending her visits to stump for Democratic candidates with Bus events at local colleges and universities. At these stops, we promoted Hillary's support for those candidates, signed up supporters, and gave out free posters.

At the University of Michigan, one Democratic student passing by was confused by our presence. "There's an election in a few weeks!"

I responded, "That's why we're here." (Why else would I visit That School Up North? Go Bucks!)

He was skeptical of my response, so he came over to chat with me. I showed him our "Ready to Vote" 2014 cards and told him that Hillary was holding a campaign rally for gubernatorial candidate Mark Schauer and now-U.S. Senator Gary Peters. "Hillary is here to support your Democratic candidates. Everyone who comes up to this table, I'm telling them to be sure to vote on November 4, this year, and support your Democratic candidates just like Hillary is."

A student standing behind this gentleman and waiting to approach me interjected: "There's an election this year?" He proved my point.

Hillary was the only person who could generate that level of enthusiasm for down-ballot Democrats in 2014. In fact, at several stops, local field organizers or county Democratic parties would set up a table next to ours, and approach Hillary supporters after they signed up with us. Supporters' enthusiasm for Hillary and the chance to get a free poster pulled them in, and we were able to direct their attention to 2014 efforts. It was one-day boost of energy and fun, complete with a big blue bus.

A field organizer for Gina Raimondo, now Governor of Rhode Island, told me that he had never signed up so many volunteers in a single shift as the night we stopped by the University of Rhode Island. He was accustomed to fellow students walking by his table and barely glancing over, but with the Hillary Bus there and the free posters, he was able to corner folks who signed up with Ready for Hillary and tell them that Hillary supports Gina, "and she could become Rhode Island's first female governor." It was perfect.

The same was true at the University of Minnesota. Campus organizers for the Democratic-Farmer-Labor Party approached everyone who signed up at our table and asked them to volunteer for U.S. Senator Al Franken and Governor Mark Dayton. "This is the best day we've ever had," one of them said. "I'm so glad you guys are here."

***

Of course, there were many 2014 factors out of our control, but that wasn't ever going to stop us from joining Hillary and doing everything we could to help our Party and its candidates. Some reporters wondered why we contributed $25,000 to Jack Hatch or Vincent Sheheen, gubernatorial candidates in Iowa and South Carolina, respectively, both facing steep uphill battles at the time of our contributions. The answer was simple: We were doing our part.

Among the candidates aided by Ready for Hillary who were victorious on Election Day are: Connecticut governor Dan Malloy, now-Michigan U.S. Senator Gary Peters, Minnesota governor Mark Dayton, Minnesota U.S. Senator Al Franken, New Hampshire governor Maggie Hassan, New Hampshire U.S. Senator Jeanne Shaheen, now-Pennsylvania governor Tom Wolf, now-Rhode Island governor Gina Raimondo, and Virginia U.S. Senator Mark Warner. We are proud to have done our part to help these and other Democrats win.

Part III: The Players

THE TEAM

The Ready for Hillary staff was one of the best teams ever assembled. Morale was high. Teamwork was a philosophy we lived by. Sure, we had the usual disagreements, but they were short-lived, and when we fought we did so like loving siblings. We also had zero leaks. We lived by three cardinal rules that came directly from Craig: 1. Do no harm. 2. Include everybody. 3. Make Hillary proud.

Ours was a team inspired by Hillary – inspired by the very idea of a *potential* Hillary Clinton candidacy. I've worked on campaigns for Kool-Aid-inducing candidates like Sherrod Brown, Ted Strickland, and Hillary herself. The candidate keeps you motivated through stressful days and late nights. Yet in our case, we had no candidate. One-third of our team had never even met Hillary. The majority of our team had never worked for her. But her life, her work, and her values were enough to keep us going every day. My colleagues and I remained devoted and determined as if she were there cheering us on at every turn. (We did have a life-size Hillary cardboard cut-out in the office watching over us).

My colleagues and I believed in the power of organizing and specifically in the power of Hillary's grassroots supporters.

***

Ready for Hillary's first national headquarters was Adam and Kirby's living room. There, they built up a social media base, stuffed envelopes, and made calls while their son Cameron, then 4 years old, could sometimes be heard screaming in the background. Kirby would later join the team in an official capacity as Deputy Operations Director.

As our team expanded, we spent some time in Rising Tide Interactive's office on 19th Street NW in Washington, with Nickie and me working out of the conference room there. When we weren't at Rising Tide, we were holding strategy sessions at whatever nearby Starbucks had a free table.

Then came an actual national headquarters, all the way outside Washington's I-495 beltway at the very last Metrorail stop on the yellow line. Getting to a meeting in the city by public transit took as long as an hour. Thankfully, if we were running late we would load up in our intern Dana Marks's Jeep Cherokee and she would drop us off. The *Washington*

Post's Phil Rucker described our headquarters as "a drab office near a nail salon and Chinese takeout restaurant outside the Beltway in Alexandria." He went on to say "the windows are painted over and the carpet is stained." Yep, that was our office!

Paint on the walls was dirty and cracked, so Adam decided to paint the entire office himself. A horrible musty smell filled the office, particularly in the basement. An actual intern duty was emptying the water collected inside the dehumidifier, which filled up about four times a day. Along with the mustiness, good karma filled the air. The office had recently been used by then-U.S. Senate candidate Tim Kaine in his successful 2012 bid. I'm pretty sure the dead mouse in the basement, lying in the middle of the staircase, was a souvenir left by Kaine campaign manager Mike Henry.

Drab as it may have been, it was the first office to support Hillary Clinton for president in 2016. One by one, TV networks started visiting. CBS went live one morning at 5AM. Often, reporters showed up unexpectedly. Whenever a photographer or videographer was present, interns would stop what they were doing and sit at the long conference tables and stuff envelopes with bumper stickers, producing stock photos and b-roll that are still used by media outlets today.

We put a great deal of effort into that office, but after only four months, our landlord who had in-kinded the space needed to rent it out to a tenant who would pay. (Reasonable). Adam then started scouting out a new location for our headquarters.

***

Searching for a new office, Adam came across a very affordable space in Arlington, Virginia's Rosslyn neighborhood. It had amazing views of Washington, including the U.S. Capitol Building and the Washington Monument. The office building was set to be torn down in a few years, by which time we would no longer need it. In the neighboring building was the headquarters of Terry McAuliffe, then a candidate for Governor of Virginia and a longtime Clinton friend.

The first reporter to visit our Rosslyn headquarters was Reid Epstein, then of POLITICO, which was headquartered across the street. We weren't ready to announce our new digs quite yet, but I made the mistake of tweeting a picture from Rosslyn's Café Asia, one of our favorite after-work locales and where we would run into our friends from the anti-Hillary group America Rising from time to time. When he visited, Reid made an off-handed remark about the turquoise color of the walls, and right on cue, Adam repainted the office walls the very next day.

Our original Rosslyn office team included Adam, Kirby, Nickie, Alissa, Alex, Eric, and Rachel. (We were the only ones lucky enough to have worked out of the Alexandria office). As we expanded in staff size, it became clear that we would need to take over an adjacent wing of the 5th Floor. Accessing the additional space required our landlord to demolish one of the walls. Posted on that wall by Adam was a sign with Reagan's famous quote ending: "Mr. Gorbachev, tear down this wall!"

Next to every light switch in the office was a picture of Hillary along with a quote from 2007: "I turn off a light and say, 'Take that, Iran,' and 'Take that, Venezuela'" followed by a note that said "Listen to Mom: Turn off the lights!" I had my then-associate Giovanni Hashimoto create these signs late one night; I was usually the last to show up at the office and the last to leave (Amy Drummond and I traded off), and I constantly had to turn off many lights.

Our constituency and field office room had a placard on it that read: "Ready for Coffee." Our conference rooms were labeled with the names of places Hillary had lived throughout her life. The Little Rock Conference Room was where we had our all-staff meetings. Others included: the Park Ridge Conference Room, the Chappaqua Conference Room, the Whitehaven Conference Room and the Wellesley Conference Room. These were just a few of the gems at Ready for Hillary headquarters. For obvious reasons, Hillary never visited, but I think she would have gotten a big kick out of it.

THE FOUR LEGS

Early on, with a multitude of Republican attacks on Hillary that were going unanswered, I felt a responsibility to respond to the attacks in kind. No one else was doing it. I pushed Adam on this many times, but he wouldn't entertain the discussion, reminding me that grassroots organizing was our focus and that was the end of the story.

I vented to Tracy while sitting outside Tippy's Taco next to our Huntington office. "Hillary's staff usually doesn't comment, and I'm not allowed to defend her at all, so who is going to defend her? Are all these attacks just going to go unanswered?!" She paused for a moment to allow me to contain myself. "Seth, you care a lot about Hillary and want to protect her," Tracy told me. "That's a good thing. It shows your dedication. But we have to think about these things strategically rather than emotionally." I wasn't sure if I had just been built up or bitch-slapped.

Tracy went on to share with me that key discussions were taking place for a rapid response operation for the purpose of defending Hillary from all the attacks. That organization, an arm of David Brock's empire, would be called Correct the Record. It would be led by Burns Strider, Isaac Wright, Adrienne Elrod and Sam Ritzman – all friends and former colleagues from 2008 who would spend each day fighting back against attacks on Hillary.

If I were asked for a response to Republicans' latest politically motivated attacks about Benghazi or anything else, I sent the reporter over to Adrienne. If it were more appropriate to showcase grassroots support than respond to an attack on Hillary, Adrienne sent that reporter my way. Teamwork.

Best of all, as I later told friends, "All I do is love Hillary, all day long, and I get paid to do it."

***

The organization that would focus on big money, big donors, and paid media was Priorities USA. It was the same super PAC that in 2012 raised $84 million to help re-elect President Obama by running blisteringly effective ads against Mitt Romney in places like Ohio. Priorities' biggest 2012 donor, Hollywood's Jeff Katzenberg, along with other key Priorities players, sought early on to transition the organization away from being President Obama's super PAC and into the big-money super PAC supporting Hillary for 2016.

Priorities USA had two phases in its relationship with Ready for Hillary. The first phase was short-lived but well-documented. As Priorities quietly planned its transition, Ready for Hillary loudly executed its launch. A collision was inevitable, and at a series of closed-door meetings some even suggested that Ready for Hillary should be shut down. Thanks to the thousands upon thousands of Hillary supporters who were not in those meetings but who had joined Ready for Hillary, that suggestion was smartly rejected.

A solution was reached: Ready for Hillary placed a cap on contributions at $25,000 – even though we could legally receive contributions of unlimited amounts. This move helped Ready for Hillary focus on its grassroots purpose, assured Priorities that they would have a lock on big checks, and freed big donors from being asked for big 2016 money amid the 2014 midterm elections.

But I don't want to confuse the initial misunderstandings between the organizations with the genuine teamwork and camaraderie that soon followed. Priorities deftly restructured its leadership and included on its Board of Directors three Ready for Hillary advisors (Allida, Harold Ickes and former Michigan governor Jennifer Granholm, who served as co-chair of the Board). In addition, Ready for Hillary developed solid relationships with Priorities' new staff, including Executive Director Buffy Wicks, under whom many Ready for Hillary staff worked previously, as well as Communications Director Peter Kauffmann (a role taken on recently by my Ohio buddy Justin Barasky). Priorities was going to do critical work if and when Hillary decided to run, and we weren't going to allow early disputes get in the way of working together.

***

EMILY's List has been an integral player from the very inception of a potential 2016 Hillary candidacy. While they don't endorse non-candidates, the launch of their Madam President project was an unprecedented initiative dedicated to electing America's first woman president – and it was pretty obvious from the beginning who that woman might be. Conducting research, polling, focus groups, and messaging,

EMILY's List was a key leg in the four-legged stool to encourage Hillary Clinton to run and prepare for her potential candidacy. Jess McIntosh, the now Vice President of Communications, Executive Director Jess O'Connell, and President Stephanie Schriock were tremendous players.

Informed by their research, EMILY's List reminded us all that the fact that Hillary was a woman was of course significant, but that we would be electing the very best qualified *person* for the job. If and when Hillary decided to run, she would obviously need to decide the extent to which she emphasized her gender. The early work of EMILY's List was essential in determining voters' attitudes toward a potential women president in 2016. The possibility of making history is very motivating to Hillary's supporters as well as potentially one of several factors that could influence swing voters, but the thought of supporting Hillary only because she is a woman was never going to be a winner for the electorate as a whole.

There was a smart nuance to Madam President. Electing a woman president was not "Hillary or bust." There were numerous women such as Kirsten Gillibrand, Amy Klobuchar, Janet Napolitano, Elizabeth Warren, and others who are absolutely qualified to be president and may one day seek to be so. Madam President is about showing that America was ready for a woman president, and American women are ready to be president. That was the case whether or not Hillary decided to run in 2016, even though she was of course the potential candidate on everyone's mind.

***

It was a "division of labor" between four organizations each doing what they did best. With our partners at Correct the Record, Priorities USA, and EMILY's List all playing their essential roles, Ready for Hillary was able to focus exclusively on ours: Building a massive list of grassroots Hillary supporters encouraging her to run and getting ready to help her win.

THE BELIEVERS

Several Clinton veterans stepped up to the plate, took a chance on a group of young operatives and believed in the power of Hillary's supporters across the country.

Craig T. Smith, Minyon Moore, Jill Alper, Tracy Sefl, Harold Ickes, Ellen Tauscher, Jennifer Granholm, Marty Chavez, Ann Lewis, Susie Tompkins Buell, Charlie Baker, Michael Whouley, David Brock, and so many other longtime Clintonites offered their encouragement and expertise.

Craig, Tracy, Harold, Ann, Marty, Ellen and Governor Granholm became official senior advisors and played invaluable roles. Others were vital behind the scenes. It was Minyon who introduced Craig to Adam and who gave us love that only Minyon can give. It was Jill who helped secure Governor Granholm and Sen. McCaskill's support. It was Charlie and Whouley who advocated for us and helped guide our politics. It was Susie Buell who established the Ready for Hillary branding. Every one of these individuals was critical to our success.

***

One of our early backers in particular needed zero convincing.

Adam texted me ecstatically one morning:

hey, do u know who Ellen Tauscher is?

Congresswoman

yes.

state too?

yes. she just gave us $2,500

whoa!

It was an eye-popping amount of money at the time, matching our largest contribution to date.

Adam then scrambled to get in touch with her and, as she tells it, he asked if she was *the* Ellen Tauscher – something she found comical. Ellen, a former congresswoman who worked with Hillary at the State Department, gave us credibility when she announced her very early support for the effort, first in the *San Francisco Chronicle* (we wanted potential donors to pay attention) and then in our very first press release announcing a prominent supporter.

The best part about Ellen's contribution was that she made it unsolicited. Just supporters across the country discovered Ready for Hillary online and signed up, she too went to our website and made a contribution. She didn't know who specifically was behind the effort, but we seemed professional and determined in her view, and we were promoting a cause she believed in. That was good enough for her.

***

I'll admit: I had no idea who Craig Smith was when Adam first threw out his name as someone who was offering us help.

There's a reason I didn't know who Craig was. He's a humble Arkansas boy who doesn't promote himself and who doesn't want his name in the press. He served as White House political director under President Clinton, and fought in the trenches for decades for a man he believes in so much. He started working for the Clintons when Bill was Attorney General of Arkansas, and in 1991 he was the first employee hired on then-Governor Clinton's presidential campaign.

Craig had a fascinating life, living in Fort Lauderdale, Florida and electing heads of state around the world while serving as our Senior Advisor. He believed in our mission from the start, when very few insiders did. He was also quite prophetic about Ready for Hillary's path, saying early on: "Everyone in DC hates this, and everyone outside of DC loves it. That's how I know it's going to be successful."

People close to Craig told us that he had never been happier in his career than during his involvement with Ready for Hillary. He saw in Ready for Hillary an idealism that was missing from too many facets of the 2008 campaign. I assume that he saw a much younger Craig in all of us as we waged this effort together. And his pride in our team was compounded by the fact that his daughter joined our team.

When people ask me for a moment in time when Ready for Hillary's success started to take off, I often cite the beginning of Craig's involvement. Of course, he would say otherwise, because even though he knows that he made a huge difference, he wouldn't want anyone giving him credit.

***

What can I say about Tracy Sefl? Or, what *couldn't* I say about Tracy Sefl?

Tracy came to Ready for Hillary by way of Ann Lewis, Communications Director in President Clinton's White House and the very first financial contributor to Ready for Hillary.

My first conversation with Tracy came on our official launch day, April 2, 2013. She reached out and asked me to give her a call. I didn't know if she was spying on us, making sure we didn't embarrass ourselves, or just graciously offering her help. At the time, it may have been a combination of the three.

I knew of this legendary woman and we were Facebook friends, but I must admit I was quite nervous in our first conversation, and I'm glad that Nickie and I had had a couple of drinks at dinner first. "Please don't think I'm stupid," I was thinking in the back of my mind as I called her. Tracy was the real deal! The next day, she was going on as a guest on CNN's The Lead hosted by Jake Tapper, and she asked what she could do to help. "Say our name, I guess… our website… I don't know…" She did, and much more articulately than me.

I often called her "TV Tracy," and Adam and I joked that her TV personality is the exact same as her real-life personality. (Her default face is a wide grin. Mine is a scowl). Even though she was an all-star and didn't need the help, she valued our opinion and would always ask for our thoughts whenever she was prepping for a TV appearance. "Thoughts welcome," she would tell us.

Every day, Tracy gave us a great deal of mainstream credibility with the media. She knew all the gossip and was able to flag brewing problems before they became actual problems. This was critical early on, but it was particularly important later as our work became more and more serious and we had a distinct responsibility to protect Hillary's brand. She became so active in Ready for Hillary's work that she eventually became a paid advisor and played an invaluable role in all of our success.

THE OBAMAITES

It was summer of 2008, well after Hillary had conceded and had thrown her support behind then-Sen. Barack Obama. An annoying email chain was exploding on the Hillary campaign alumni listserv. Apparently someone made a movie about how the Obama campaign was a bunch of meanies, and the movie prompted a lot of useless rantings from fellow alums.

"Why can't he be nice to her?" one former field organizer asked, referring to our Party's nominee-in-waiting.

Not surprisingly, the chain was leaked to journalist Marc Ambinder. I immediately sent the link to Marc's post to the listserv telling people to stop being stupid, and I offered up this important quote from Hillary's June 2008 concession speech at the National Building Museum:

"Life is too short, time is too precious and the stakes are too high to dwell on what might have been. We need to come together to achieve what still can be."

Hillary's words were as true in 2008 as they were when looking toward 2016, and, leading by example, Ready for Hillary sought to live by those words every day.

***

Asking for the support of President Obama's earliest backers was of course strategic for us diehard Clinton operatives, but it was also simply the right thing to do. Every Hillary 2016 supporter had a role to play in this movement. "You can't fight the last battle," Craig often reminded supporters. "You have to fight the next battle."

Not every Hillary diehard agreed. The gripes went like this: "I voted for Hillary last time and I'm still angry about what happened!" One supporter in Kansas City even told me: "I write in Hillary's name for president every chance I get!" (Because *that's* helpful).

"We need to look *forward*," I told a woman in Texas, after she lamented about the 2008 primary and what she described as the poor treatment of Hillary supporters in her particular caucus. "Take that frustration and use it for good," I encouraged her, "but don't blame the President or his supporters."

***

I once felt their pain, having been one of two opposition researchers on Hillary's 2008 campaign dissecting then-Sen. Obama's record. It wasn't a high-ranking position by any means, but it was one that consumed me to such a level that I was removed from reality. I had to come up with a laundry list of often-superficial arguments of why then-Sen. Obama shouldn't be president.

Sam Ritzman, who became Research Director for Correct the Record, was my partner in that campaign. We sometimes knew then-Sen. Obama's record better than he knew it himself. In March of 2007, we traveled to Springfield and Chicago, collecting records and digging into the past of the former state senator. We poured through microfiches of his state senate votes, scoped out where he got his haircuts, and drove by his Hyde Park home – then unprotected by Secret Service – just for due diligence's sake. Creepy, right?

Amidst the Lexis-Nexis dumps, bullet-writing, and searching for every possible reason in the world why this man was "Not Ready for Prime Time" (as my master research document was titled), I finally allowed myself to come to reality: then-Sen. Obama was a truly worthy and well-qualified rival. He would become an incredible president – and appoint a great secretary of state.

***

Years had gone by, Hillary joined his team, and the President deserved all of our support. And yet some people still couldn't get past that 2008 primary.

Did these folks think they were somehow better Hillary supporters because they didn't get on board with President Obama? Were they on another planet when both Hillary and President Clinton campaigned for him? Did they miss that whole Secretary of State thing?

***

When Adam was asked why he and Allida founded Ready for Hillary, one of the reasons he cited was the sheer number of President Obama's early 2008 supporters who approached him as Hillary was stepping down as Secretary of State. They asked him what they could do "right now" to make her our next president. We needed their time, talents, and expertise. And we needed them to know that the Clinton Door was wide open.

Enter Jeremy Bird and Mitch Stewart.

The addition of their firm, 270 Strategies, to Ready for Hillary's effort was an ultimate coup, and the 270 team was instrumental to the movement's success every step of the way. There was never an ounce of animosity between 270 and the '08 Hillary diehards who were part of Ready for Hillary. We were the same team.

Jeremy and Mitch, architects of President Obama's 2008 and 2012 victories, were tremendous assets. Lauren Kidwell, and later, Gabby Seay, were unsung heroes, working with us daily and helped craft our strategic field and constituency plans to harness the energy of grassroots supporters in every corner of the country. Lynda Tran, Hari Sevugan, and Eleis Brennan were a huge help to me in communications, particularly framing big national pieces. And I must say that 270 really liked the attention they got from our partnership. "Have Mitch do it" was our default response if an important interview request came in. It was such a win-win.

This wasn't about dollar signs for them. They believed in the mission of Ready for Hillary. In fact, they believed in it so much that they went through the difficult step of reaching out to Vice President Biden's office to discuss the prospective contract. Empowering supporters and fostering a movement were instinctual to the early Obama folks, while Hillary's 2008 decision-makers neglected and at times even publicly ridiculed these same tactics. A quiet goal of Ready for Hillary was to right the wrongs of 2008, and 270 Strategies helped us achieve that goal each day.

***

Much like the early addition of 270 Strategies to our team, the announcement of the first member of Congress to support Ready for Hillary sent shockwaves around the chattering class of Washington. "Holy s***," Tracy responded to Adam upon hearing the news of our upcoming announcement. It was huge indeed, and it had all the salacious elements of a perfect Washington story.

Enter Claire McCaskill.

This announcement was framed by some as a bury-the-hatchet attempt by Sen. McCaskill to get on the Clintons' good side after saying some not-nice things about President Clinton in 2006 and endorsing then-Sen. Obama in 2008. To us, though, her support symbolized the journey of millions of early Obama supporters at the grassroots level who wanted Hillary Clinton to be the next president. Prior to the big announcement, I had a great conversation with Claire's communications director John LaBombard, in which he described how his boyfriend was a diehard 2008 Hillary supporter and he was a diehard 2008 Obama supporter. Everything had come full circle for John, his boss, and so many others.

David Freedlander of the Daily Beast described this unification of former rival teams as an "orgy." There was a good amount of truth to that description, and Ready for Hillary's millions of supporters – many of them early Obamaites – created the environment to make it so.

THE MEDIA

A book on media relations – if I were to write one – would be titled *A Tale of Two Bathrooms*.

New York Times reporter Amy Chozick chronicled an incident in which she was followed to the bathroom by a handler watching her every move at a Clinton entity's event.

Months later, at the Harkin Steak Fry, there was a shortage of bathrooms on the Balloon Fields, so I went ahead and tweeted:

"Reporters: You are free to use the bathroom on @thehillarybus."

A flurry of retweets ensued. Bloomberg's Mark Halperin replied to ask if we had magazines for them. We didn't have magazines, but we did have toilet paper and hand sanitizer. Reporters from ABC, Bloomberg, CNN, *The Hill*, MSNBC, NBC, POLITICO and other outlets used our facilities, some of them multiple times throughout the day. (I won't call out the specific reporters, as tempting as that may be).

Nearly a year after it occurred, the Chozick Bathroom Incident was still fresh on the minds of the press corps. "Are you going to follow me to the bathroom today?" more than one reporter asked upon arriving at the Ready for Hillary National Finance Council Meeting at the Sheraton in New York City. Coincidentally, our meeting took place at the exact location, exact floor, exact bathrooms, exact everything, as the event chronicled by Amy.

While official meeting sessions of that Finance Council meeting were closed to the media, we did the next best thing for reporters: we set up a media workspace and brought in a string of insiders to address different topics in a rolling press avail. Throughout the day, reporters were welcome to use the bathrooms unattended, get coffee and talk to donors. After all, if reporters wanted to get any of these donors on the phone separately from this meeting, they would have the capacity to do so. Why not make everyone's life a little easier?

The strategy paid off. Articles were positive, reporters were happy, and the world was perfect. Peter Nicholas of the *Wall Street Journal* took to Twitter after the meeting, offering "kudos" to our staff for the professionalism with which we treated the press. Others followed suit. By the end of the day, the press corps and our staff were such besties that we made an on-the-spot decision to invite them to our post-meeting reception.

***

Adam, Craig, Tracy, and I lived by the philosophy that if you treat reporters well, good things will happen. Press coverage of Ready for Hillary was about 95 percent positive.

Our supporters in the states, like Terry Shumaker and Jerry Crawford, were supportive and even insistent on the media-friendly strategy, and they were instrumental in implementing it. I introduced them, along with several others in early states including Bonnie Campbell, Tyler Olsen, Jim Demers, Bakari Sellers, and others to members of the national press corps, and I didn't script them; I let them develop their own relationships with these reporters and state in their own words why they were involved with Ready for Hillary.

We gave beat reporters full access to our headquarters. We invited them to strategy sessions, organizing meetings, house parties and low-dollar fundraisers. Adam would go on the record with any outlet that asked. We authorized our constituency directors and regional field staff to go on the record to tout their programs. We were respectful of reporters amid any conflict or bad stories. The results spoke for themselves.

In addition to the media-friendly approach, we took advantage of the fact that the average Clinton beat reporter is in his or her late 20s and thus, they gave Hillaryland an opportunity for a fresh start. Many of these reporters barely remember Whitewater or the Lincoln Bedroom, and they haven't been in journalism long enough to be having PTSD from the 2008 campaign. They were fresh-eyed and ready to give Hillary a chance, and they were happy that an organization with "Hillary" in its name was giving them a chance as well.

***

Aside from Tracy, a recent George Washington University grad from Buffalo named Sean England rounded out our press shop. Sean was dedicated, talented beyond his age, and had a great attitude. He had worked with press teams in Senator Schumer's office as well as the White

House. He developed relationships with Clinton beat reporters and traveled across the country. I could count on him to think on his feet and handle any situation. He loved working national reporters (I always joked with him that he had a huge crush on one in particular) but was not above doing grunt work, either.

Sean, Tracy, and I juggled requests from everyone from the *Washington Post* to the *Daily Iowan* to the *Keene Sentinel* and Swedish radio. The international outlets were particularly demanding ("Hillary is SO popular in our country," said every international reporter always…) and because of their requests, I half-jokingly made Sean our "international press secretary."

Indeed, Hillary was loved around the world, and the twenty-or-so requests we received from international outlets every week were a testament to that. At one point we had such a backlog of international media requests that I told Sean to schedule an open house. An Epcot Center of journalists flooded in, leaving no less than four hours later. Some of our non-press colleagues decided to keep their doors closed from then on whenever a reporter visited. Jessica Grounds was always a good sport, giving interviews to any international media outlet that dropped by.

While it's easy as a communications operative to dismiss international journalists, the fact is that many Americans get their news from international sources. Ready for Hillary's supporters abroad and inside the country urged us to make sure that international journalists were part of our outreach. A Korean journalist stopped by our first headquarters one day to write a story about our operation. After talking to our staff, he sat down and stuffed envelopes with our interns, volunteering for the rest of the day.

Treat the press well, and good things happen.

Part IV: The States

IOWA

Nowhere in the country was it more important that we get our politics right than in the State of Iowa. Hillary's 2008 Iowa campaign was a dark chapter in recorded history. Hillaryland's distaste for the caucus system in 2008 was no secret. Her top 2008 campaign advisers had even belittled young Iowans who were caucusing for the first time.

Yet for as much of a disaster as Hillary's 2008 Iowa effort was portrayed to be, it was at the same time incredibly successful, if not historic, and she had more support in the state than what the punditry gave her credit. In fact, she had more people caucus for her in 2008 than had caucused for any other candidate on either side of the aisle in the history of the Iowa Caucus. (Of course, then-Senators Obama and Edwards also achieved that mark, but that detail doesn't discount the 70,000 or so Iowans who came out to support her that night, over 150 percent more than had caucused for any other candidate prior or since).

Despite Hillary's support in the state, we knew there would be no free ride for any candidate. And we knew we had to show her all of the support she had in a state where some would have you believe that she had no support at all.

***

As we began to organize in the state, we gathered a kitchen cabinet of 2008 Hillary and 2008 Obama supporters. Craig's first call was to Jerry Crawford. Jerry had served as State Director of President Clinton's Iowa campaigns in 1992 and 1996, and in 2008 he was Hillary's Midwest Co-Chair. His two goals right now in life are, according to the *Washington Post*, "delivering Iowa for Hillary Clinton and winning the Kentucky Derby." (He owns horses. Ask him about them if you get the chance). Jerry, with help from his then-law clerk Blake Hanson, helped us get started in Iowa.

Bonnie Campbell served as Iowa's Attorney General and ran a strong but unsuccessful for Governor in 1994. She was a longtime Clinton supporter who knew all too well that Iowa didn't have a great track record when it came to electing women – no woman had ever won the Iowa Caucuses, no woman had ever been elected Governor, no woman had ever been elected

U.S. Senator by that time, and no woman had ever been elected to the U.S. House of Representatives.

Just as important as getting longtime Hillary supporters on board was getting Obama early Obama supporters on board as well. To achieve that goal, Mitch Stewart of 270 Strategies was instrumental. He had served as Director of Field Operations during then-Sen. Obama's 2008 Iowa campaign and introduced us to activists across the state. State Rep. Tyler Olsen, also an early Obama backer, was another key player in everything we did in the state. Jackie Norris, then-Sen. Obama's 2008 Caucus Director, was on board, joining in meetings and conference calls with her past counterpart, the always energetic Teresa Vilmain.

***

"Get me one of those $1 double cheeseburgers," Craig told Alissa and I at 2:00AM as we stopped at a Burger King en route to Iowa. His eyes were barely open as he popped his head up from the back seats of the SUV we had hastily rented. Our flight out of Chicago O'Hare to Des Moines was cancelled because of heavy snow, as was our back-up flight that we nearly boarded from Chicago Midway. We had to drive overnight and hopefully sleep for two hours before conducting a series of critical meetings the next day. Stakes for this trip were high and it wasn't going well so far. To top it off, my bag got lost, so I would be showing up to these meetings wearing the same casual clothes I had worn on the plane.

Craig had just returned from some far-off country doing God-knows-what and hadn't slept in 36 hours, but he was going to get as much sleep as he could in the back of the SUV and then power through the next day. He had a Hillaryesque ability to hop on a flight anywhere in the world, immediately conduct meetings, come back, take care of business back home, fly somewhere else, and address a completely different set of challenges, gliding effortlessly through global and domestic political obstacles. It was fascinating to observe.

Anyhow, we got Craig that $1 sandwich he wanted, but it ran us a whole $1.69(!). "Don't tell Craig. He will never let it go," I commanded of Alissa as we hobbled back to the SUV through the snow. Adam finished his cigarette, and we continued our 50 mile-per-hour drive on I-80 West.

***

We set up an entire day of meetings with public officials, labor leaders, Hillary '08 supporters, and Obama '08 supporters. Anyone was welcomed to attend any session, and some supporters stayed all day while others came and went. The meetings were held at Exile Brewing Company, and the restaurant staff whipped up some amazing lasagna. Adam and I had the opportunity to reunite with 2008 campaign friends like Brenda Kole and Micah Honeycutt who came out to show their support.

We faced a difficult decision of whether or not to invite media to the meetings. My inclination was not to invite them, so as to allow attendees to speak openly and freely. But I ultimately wanted to defer to Iowans. "We don't want this to be the same old Clinton campaign," Teresa said. "Let's invite them."

Two national reporters – Phil Rucker from the *Washington Post* and Ruby Cramer from BuzzFeed – joined us as the Iowa press corps came out in force. Meeting legends like longtime Iowa reporters James Lynch and Kay Henderson was a very humbling experience. I was just another out-of-state Democratic operative, while they were veterans who had covered the Iowa Caucuses for decades. I had two strategies: Be humble, and play up my Ohio roots. I could make small talk about B1G Football and how East Coast-ers think our states are the same place.

Not everyone who attended the meetings was on board with Ready for Hillary. That was okay; we were there to have a conversation and get feedback. Not everyone's feedback was the positive, and State Senator Janet Peterson in particular made some constructive points. "What you're asking in terms of creating lists is not what Iowans want," she said, quoted by BuzzFeed. "You guys want a list. Iowans want a sense of engagement and conversation and dialogue like they got on the Obama campaign." She was right. And Craig was right in his response: The one thing we couldn't provide was a candidate.

But one thing we knew we could do, and were more determined than ever to do, was to activate Hillary supporters to help the Iowa Democratic Party and Democratic candidates throughout the state.

***

By the day of the Harkin Steak Fry, we had organized in all of Iowa's 99 counties. This was no easy task. Our colleague Gabi Kahn stepped up and coordinated a Ready for Hillary presence at 84 of the 99 county conventions that had taken place months before. She had a big Iowa county map in her office that was constantly being updated. Our Deputy Midwest Regional Organizing Director Gracie Brandsgard set up house parties in a few of the remaining counties. Gabi identified activists in a few additional counties and sent them materials for clipboarding and tabling events.

We had five counties remaining the week of the big event, and having come so close, it became critical – even imperative – that we finish the job of organizing and identifying enthusiastic supporters in all 99 counties. Our digital associate Evan Wessel and I were in Iowa early for the Steak Fry. We took my white rental car and put Ready for Hillary placards around it to make it look like a Hot Rod, using an X-Acto knife to allow a continuous stripe of placards while maintaining functioning doors. We called this car the "Little Hillary Bus." Evan and I then proceeded to drive from county to county, in two days of thunder and rain, finding places in the various counties to sign up supporters. For good measure, I took pictures of him standing with an umbrella in front of county welcome signs. Evan later said this book should "embellish the tornadoes on our 12-hour drive." I don't remember tornado reports, but we probably would have done those trips regardless.

***

The 37th Annual Harkin Steak Fry was a big deal. Not only was it Senator Harkin's last Steak Fry after six terms in the U.S. Senate, it was Hillary's first appearance in Iowa since the 2008 caucuses and her first appearance on the campaign trail of the 2014 cycle. The significance of this event could not be overstated.

Adam went all out. We had placards. We had 4 foot by 8 foot signs. We had cherry pickers. We had the Hillary Bus. We had a U-Haul. We had buses picking up college students across the state. We had t-shirts. We had fans. We had just about everything. We had a contingent of about 70 – a mix of staff and volunteers like Al Perez and Karen Murphy – staying at the Des Moines Marriot. Marty Chavez, a longtime Clinton supporter, former mayor of Albuquerque and Ready for Hillary senior advisor, played the role of chaperone and gave rides from the Des Moines airport. Adam flew them all in from across the country partly as a reward for their strong support and partly to make sure we could do our part in executing a successful Steak Fry worthy of Sen. Harkin's distinguished career. Wearing bright green "VOLUNTEER" shirts, our contingent worked side by side with local volunteers to prepare the Balloon Fields for the event, including hanging up alternating, oversized Harkin, Hatch, Braley and "READY" signs.

Thousands of rally signs, paid for by Ready for Hillary, were held up across the Balloon Fields on the day of the Steak Fry. Missing from the signs was the word "Hillary," because this day was about honoring Senator Harkin's legacy and supporting Iowa Democrats' efforts for the 2014 election. Instead of our usual "I'm Ready for Hillary," these rally signs said "Thank You, Tom!" and "Thank You, Ruth!" The latter was to recognize Tom's wife, a powerhouse in her own right. On the back of these Tom and Ruth signs was "READY TO VOTE."

Frank Chi, our videographer, made an incredible video ending with supporters of all walks of life, including a young girl who said Hillary showed women "we're not just something in the background. 'You can dooooo thiiiis!!'" The video ended with this beautiful line from Hillary: "It's time to heed the push of our values and the pull of our future. It's time to write that new chapter in the American dream." Though her speech was about Tom and Iowa Democrats, to her supporters it was almost as if she were announcing her candidacy right there from that stage.

After Hillary's speech, President Clinton spoke. It was a tradition for former presidents to speak last, but as he took the stage, some attendees began to exit. Poor Bill! He may have been president, but his wife was the main attraction. Earlier in the day, President Clinton was asked by ABC's Jonathan Karl what he thought of all of the Ready for Hillary staff and supporters joining the Steak Fry. The response was one only Bill Clinton could give: "Amazing. They are amazing. You know I saw some of them here… They're like Energizer Bunnies. They're just everywhere."

Word spread like wildfire to our volunteers across the Balloon Fields: "President Clinton just called us Energizer Bunnies!"

***

After the Steak Fry, our Young Americans Director Rachel Schneider and I embarked on a Hillary Bus tour of six Iowa colleges and universities:

Iowa State University, the University of Iowa, Drake University, Cornell College, the University of Northern Iowa, and Grinnell College. MSNBC's Alex Seitz-Wald joined us for the Iowa State University stop and profiled one of our student leaders. Eric joined us for the first two stops.

At the University of Iowa, Eric had an epic strategy: Stand on top of the Bus with a bullhorn and call out individual students until they come over and sign up. Among his lines: "Hey guy in the hoodie! Is that a protein shake? Do you want a poster?"

At Drake University, we weren't able to park the Bus close to any campus foot traffic, so Eric pulled up his rental truck and stood atop it, in his absolute element calling students over to sign up.

"I like your purse. Do you want a poster?" He had the whole campus laughing.

For Cornell College, we had exactly one – one! – "cornellcollege.edu" domain email address in our database prior to arrival. Rachel reached out to this young woman, who promptly got back to her and secured a prime spot for the Bus. Those two signed up 113 students on a campus of 1,100 – that's more than 10 percent of the student body – in a matter of two hours. One supporter became 113. Now that's some amazing organizing!

***

State Senator Peterson's concerns were well founded. The flags that she raised made us determined to do everything we could to help Iowa Democrats in 2014. We wanted to contribute something rather than take something. While we didn't have a candidate, but we had a lot of supporters and some money to spend. We made direct contributions to candidates including a $25,000 contribution to gubernatorial candidate Jack Hatch. All of our engagement and activity in Iowa center around helping in the 2014 elections. Goodwill resulted, both for us and for the woman we supported.

"Everyone out here really sings your praises," a POLITICO reporter texted me from Iowa as Ready for Hillary's effort was winding down.

NEW HAMPSHIRE

New Hampshire is indeed Clinton Country. That was clear to me ever since I stepped foot in the state.

Terry Shumaker, a former ambassador and top Clinton supporter, played a lead role in our efforts in the state. He actually had the opportunity to go with then-First Lady of Arkansas Hillary Clinton in 1991 to file then-Governor Clinton's signatures to get him on the ballot for the New Hampshire primary, which would make Bill the "Comeback Kid." Additional members of our New Hampshire kitchen cabinet were Ned Helms and Jim Demers, co-chairs of then-Sen. Obama's 2008 New Hampshire team. Jim was famously called out by Hillary during a 2008 debate because he is a state lobbyist, and the role of lobbyists was an issue in the campaign. No hard feelings, Jim said on MSNBC; that's politics and he never took it personally. He was all-in for Hillary this time.

***

In January 2014, Craig, Alissa, and I caught a direct flight from Washington to Manchester, a flight that exists for the obvious purpose to quickly transport political operatives and reporters to the state.

Lots of snow appropriately awaited our arrival. I was driving the rental car from the airport and Craig was in the back, pointing out all of the one-star hotels along the way and asking why we weren't staying at them. Terry met us early the next morning at our hotel, and we spent the day meeting with activists, labor leaders, and public officials, asking for their input on how we could best organize in the state and help in Democratic efforts.

I also had the opportunity to chat with the Statehouse press corps in Concord. Their Statehouse office is tiny, with five or six reporters from four media outlets crammed into a small room, desks pushed up against each other. But it's located prominently on the ground floor and gives them access to the hundreds and hundreds and hundreds of state legislators passing by. Similar to my experience in Iowa, it was humbling to chat with them about the history of the first-in-the-nation primary and all the candidates that they had met along the way. But I had one burning question for them in particular: "How did Hillary win the 2008 primary?"

Their answer was simple: "She earned it." And while many people across the country were shocked by the results on that amazing Election Night, these reporters were not surprised at all. They know their stuff and they knew to ignore the polls and buckle up for an interesting night.

We ended the visit with a big Q&A event at the Puritan Backroom, owned by the family of Chris Pappas, an Executive Councilor in New Hampshire. It was my favorite restaurant in the state. Sean Downey, himself based out of Manchester, said to me: "You know we have other places to eat, right?" Yes, yes. But no other restaurant served up the Pappas chicken tenders with honey or delectable Snickers mudslides. So good!

***

During a later visit to Manchester, driving the Hillary Bus with Sean England as my co-pilot, we were approaching our event location and noticed children literally running down the sidewalk chasing the Bus with little American flags as if Hillary herself were coming to town.

***

In March 2014, I took a very memorable trip to Keene, NH, about 60 miles West of Concord. Keene's downtown was a filming location for the movie "Jumanji," interestingly enough. Ricia McMahon, a former state representative and Clinton administration alum in the U.S. Department of Health and Human Services and the Office of National Drug Control Policy, gave me a ride. She is as much a superstar as she is a sweetheart.

We were headed to a house party at the home of acclaimed Granite State activist JoAnn Fenton. House parties are an organizing staple in New Hampshire, and I could see why.

I loved getting to know JoAnn and the long, special history of the Clintons and Keene. She had five or so framed photos taken with President and Hillary Clinton, all sitting prominently side-by-side in her living room. JoAnn asked me about an eye-popping quote in the *New Yorker* in which an anonymous (of course!) Clinton aide said Ready for Hillary amounted to "Not a single f***ing thing." The article was by then months old, but the quote still fresh on her mind because she disagreed with it so much, she believed in our mission, and she was working hard to organize in the Granite State.

We didn't need the potty-mouthed aide on our side. We had people like JoAnn, in places like Keene, and that's all that mattered.

As the house party began, people started filing in the door, 80 in total. Everyone packed into her living room, standing room only and many listening from the hallway. JoAnn spoke, followed by State Senator Molly Kelly, a longtime Clinton supporter, and me. Seated front and center on the couch was Ella Nilsen, a young reporter from the *Keene Sentinel* who wrote a great article about the event.

***

During the last four days of the 2014 campaign, we scheduled the Hillary Bus to be in the Granite State. New Hampshire, not coincidentally, was Hillary's last campaign stop for the 2014 elections. (Iowa, at the Harkin Steak Fry, was the first). There were several key races on the ballot, including Sen. Jeanne Shaheen's and Gov. Maggie Hassan's re-election bids. We printed rally signs that said "Ready for Jeanne" and "Ready for Maggie" to play off of the Ready for Hillary moniker.

The Sunday before Election Day was Hillary's big rally for Jeanne and Maggie, on a blistering cold morning in Nashua. We parked the Bus on site, and a few reporters joined us on there to keep warm. The Saint Anselm Students for Hillary team stopped by a snapped a photo. We didn't give out any Ready for Hillary signs; instead, we stuck to the Jeanne and Maggie ones. The signs were blowing away in the November wind, but Sean Downey had it all under control.

On Monday and Tuesday, we had a single objective: Get as many students to vote as possible. We spent much of Monday at Dartmouth College before heading the University of New Hampshire in Durham.

On Election Day, two Teamsters were dispatched by Ready for Hillary to drive students to the polls from a pick-up location where we were also giving out posters to grab students' attention and ask if they had voted. Students were lining up faster than we could take them, and we didn't want a single one of them to lose interest. I asked Downey if he thought I should start giving rides to the polls in the Hillary Bus. He was all about it, and I knew better than to ask Adam or Alissa for permission. So, I put a Ready for Jeanne and a Ready for Maggie placard inside the front windshield of the Bus and started packing in students and giving rides.

The Durham polling location was about a two-mile walk from campus, so it was a good thing we were there. Many students shared that they never would have voted were it not for their rides on the Hillary Bus. Tom Steyer's polar bears and reindeer were also out in full force, reminding students about the importance of climate change. I had the best time honking at the empty Scott Brown bus each time I passed it. In the end, Durham was Ready for Jeanne and Ready for Maggie, giving these candidates 69 and 70 percent of the vote, respectively, and contributing to their close-but-convincing statewide wins.

***

Every visit to New Hampshire was more gratifying than the last. Terry was proudest of anyone for what Ready for Hillary built across the country and particularly in New Hampshire.

"Someone should write a book about this," he once told me.

SOUTH CAROLINA

I loved going to South Carolina, not just because of the weather but because of the longtime and new Hillary supporters throughout the state. Wounds from the 2008 primary had healed, and the problems that many in Washington thought Hillary would have in the Palmetto State were not reflected by the sentiment on the ground. The fact is that South Carolina Democrats have always had an affection for a certain former southern governor and his wife. They just happened to go for another history-making candidate in the 2008 primary.

***

Quentin was a native of Greenville, South Carolina and one of the first in-state hires on then-Sen. Obama's 2008 campaign. He had a good lay of the land in his home state, and when he said that Black voters in South Carolina were in Hillary's corner, it wasn't political spin; it was first-hand knowledge.

State Rep. Bakari Sellers was elected to the state legislature in 2006 at the age of 22, becoming the youngest black elected official in the country. He was a big supporter of ours in the state and as a communications guy, I was one of his biggest fans. He was a young, black elected official from South Carolina who had been the first member of the legislature to endorse then-Sen. Obama in 2007.

One South Carolina Democrat who does not support Hillary described the Ready for Hillary movement as a "fan club for a boy band" and a "cult." Those were badges of honor as far as we were concerned!

***

My initial trip to South Carolina was for the State Democratic Party Convention. There was a women's breakfast the next morning at which the convention's keynote speaker would announce his support for Hillary's potential run. This was going to be an earth-shattering endorsement for Washington's chattering class, something we knew and prepared for. Tim Kaine, a U.S. Senator, former Virginia governor, former Richmond mayor, former DNC chairman, early Obama supporter, fluent Spanish speaker, Christian missionary, was the newest supporter to join the Ready for Hillary movement. Suffice it to say that I make no secret

Hillary should choose him as her running mate, if she gets that opportunity.

I had prepped reporters in advance that the news was coming. They had lines from his speech and all of the information they needed. It was going to be one of those awesome news days and we had worked closely with Tim, his Chief-of-Staff Mike Henry (deputy campaign manager of Hillary's 2008 bid), and Amy Dudley, his Communications Director, to make it all happen just right.

But sometimes things don't happen as planned. Someone not on Ready for Hillary or Sen. Kaine's staff leaked word to U.S. News & World Report's Dave Catanese of the endorsement and he ran with it. I saw the carefully planned news embargo fall apart in front of my face. I told reporters that the embargo had been lifted, and a few asked if and how the information was leaked. "Nooooo it wasn't a leak," I told them. "People are just REALLY excited!" The leak didn't matter in the end. Coverage was amazing, and how could it not be?

While strolling around Columbia and talking to Associated Press reporter Ken Thomas our perspective on the significance of Sen. Kaine's support, I stumbled upon the South Carolina Statehouse and, yes, the Confederate Flag in front. I stared at it in disbelief as I made a few more calls. Thankfully, politicians of both parties in South Carolina have since done the right thing.

***

Rachel was warned before we arrived at Clemson University that it was a very conservative campus – and indeed, a gun group on campus tweeted that our Bus was "within range" of their booth at the Student Activities Fair. Even at supposedly conservative campuses, support for Hillary was strong. We signed up 176 students at Clemson, even before classes started. The Hillary Bus even took the ALS Ice Bucket Challenge from its prime parking spot.

***

Avery and I made the trip to the Blue Jamboree in North Charleston, which was keynoted by former Michigan governor Jennifer Granholm. It's the second-largest Democratic gathering in the state, and Ready for

Hillary helped the South Carolina Dems secure her as a speaker to boost ticket sales and ensure good time for all. She even got to tour the Hillary Bus, which I assured her was American- and union-made. The former governor of Michigan deserved no less!

She put on a great performance, even invoking her signature Dr. Seuss impression, reciting in part:

"But 'round the bend, the Rs are already afraid --
I predict Dems hold the White House for another decade.
You know why the Rs quake in their boots?
'Cuz y'all will be signing up lots of recruits!
In 2016, ol' Jeb won't save the day.
Too many Bushes, his mama did say.
So the GOP's auditioning every conservative star -
Looks like their fielding another full clown car.
Rand Paul, Rick Perry, Donald Trump blowing his horn:
Just put up your feet and break out the popcorn.
We'll just let them steep in their party of tea:
And we'll fight for the White House from Detroit to SC!
Oh yes, we're amassing our Democratic artillery,
Because you know that we'll be Ready for Hillary!
For SC and Michigan our candidate could be heaven sent,
No finer words, it seems, than "Madam President."

And sure, we knew Bakari and Vincent Sheheen, the Democratic nominee for governor, and other Democrats on the ballot faced an uphill battle. That's the reality of politics in South Carolina. But they deserved our support as much as the Democratic tickets Iowa, New Hampshire, or Nevada.

***

Sometimes, just showing up and asking for support is all that it takes. We had a big imprint on the state and Hillary's support there. Don't take it from me; the *New York Times'* Maggie Haberman tweeted in May, "In Columbia, SC, not-insignificant number of former Obama backers from 08 who said Ready for Hillary reached out and brought them on board."

NEVADA

Nevada. I wish I had the opportunity to spend more time in the state. But from my limited time there, I can tell you that Hillary's support from Culinary Workers, Latinos, AAPI, LGBTQ and young Nevadans is strong.

***

Deputy Communications Director Sean England and I set out on the Hillary Bus from Vegas to Reno, leaving early and arriving late. The 12-hour jaunt was absolutely incredible. We stopped often to take pictures of the Bus with the landscapes of Nevada beauty.

We stayed at a Reno casino, stumbling upon Burning Man, where, according to its website, "tens of thousands of people gather in Nevada's Black Rock Desert to create Black Rock City, a temporary metropolis dedicated to community, art, self-expression, and self-reliance."

The next morning, we uncovered the Bus and headed to the University of Nevada, Reno. As we pulled in, a local cameraman was waiting for us, so I had Sean jump out and do the stand-up interview to distract from my impending parking job. We bought pizza for the table and, as the UNR Wolf Pack Marching Band walked by en route to rehearsal, I told Sean to get the sousaphone section to come over and take a picture with the Bus. They stopped by after rehearsal, we took some great shots and we even had them march around in front of the Bus and play their fight song.

***

The University of Nevada, Las Vegas is a great place to bring a political bus. The administration allowed us to drive right up to the main strip of campus, where cars are not allowed. Driving over numerous curbs to get there was tricky, but the Hillary Bus was up to the task.

Rachel was reunited with her friend Dante, with whom she had worked closely on President Obama's re-election campaign in the state. Dante, along with a few other UNLV students, joined us at the table on a scorching Vegas September day. We pulled out the awning to provide some shade and signed up 200 students to join the Ready for Hillary movement.

***

"I'll be the guy driving the big blue Hillary Bus in a tank top and shades," I boasted proudly to a more than few people in Vegas before the LGBTQ Pride Parade. If you've got it, flaunt it, they say, and I had a Hillary Bus to flaunt to everyone in Vegas.

We only drove in one Pride parade (Hillary's book tour coincided with Pride month), but wow, was it fun. It was also Western Regional Organizing Director Jessica Mejia's birthday, so as we waited, I sent Sean out with my credit card to get some booze for a pre-parade celebration with her.

I stayed sober for the drive, of course, and it was a good thing that I was on high alert along the Parade route as hordes of LGBTQ Nevadans and straight allies rushed toward the moving Bus to take pictures.

As I followed slowly behind the float of 99-percent-naked "firemen" in front of me, two individuals successfully opened the door and boarded the Bus while it was moving. Not wanting to start a trend, we stopped and asked them to step off.

Sean and Jessica then began walking alongside the Bus, holding up our #READY posters. Jessica entertained the firemen while Sean guarded the door to the bus so we could maintain some safety. It didn't do the trick.

Sean ran frantically over to the driver's side window. "Seth! There is a dude riding on the ladder in the back," Sean told me, laughing.

"I'm stopping right now. Tell him to get down," I responding, half-laughing but half-terrified.

This is the LGBTQ community's love for Hillary: If you see a bus with Hillary's name on it, get on that bus any way you can. Could any other political figure in America illicit this kind of reaction? Not a chance. The Bus, in many ways, was a symbol of the Ready for Hillary movement. Millions were eager to get on board.

Along the way, I blasted Katy Perry (duh!) to the crowd, honked and even waved a flag a few times when it was safe to do so.

As the parade route ended, the announcer shouted to the crowd, "Are you Ready for Hillary?" Thundering applause followed.

OHIO

"As Ohio goes, so goes the nation." –Anonymous

I know it's not an "early state," but you seriously didn't think I would leave out Ohio did you? My home state played a special role in the Ready for Hillary movement. The first Ready for Hillary paid staffer? Ohio. The first group of grassroots activists to write a letter encouraging Hillary to run? Ohio. The first member of the U.S. House of Representatives to publicly back Ready for Hillary? Ohio.

Our initial meeting with Congressman Tim Ryan was set up by Tommy Sowers, former Assistant Secretary for Public and Intergovernmental Affairs at the United States Department of Veterans Affairs. Tommy had pushed us to focus on younger, fresher pro-Hillary voices as surrogates for Ready for Hillary. And he had the perfect idea: Having Tim Ryan, his yoga and meditation buddy, be our first official supporter from the U.S. House of Representatives.

Tim is a diehard populist champion who talks with a lot of credibility about Hillary's progressive values and record. He comes from the Mahoning Valley, an area of historically declining population and declining manufacturing jobs, but a region that is now holding steady thanks in large part to Democrats' leadership and the rescue of the American auto industry. The people of the Valley, like the Congressman they elected, are resilient. Tim and his staffer, Matt Kaplan, were Ready for Hillary's biggest fans.

Tim's unwavering support was similar to the support we received across the Buckeye State. When I reached out to contacts who I hadn't talked to in years, I never had to ask if they supported Hillary. In Ohio, it was practically a given. I simply asked if they wanted to get involved with a Ready for Hillary event. And almost always, they said yes. I asked them to jump and they asked how high.

Ohio is Hillary Country.

***

We understand in Ohio that successful presidential efforts are not built overnight. They are built over time and from the ground up. When talking about why the work of Ready for Hillary was so important, I used this Ohio example: After President Obama made history in 2008, his supporters didn't stop organizing. His operation geared up for 2012 by engaging volunteers in the 2009 push for Obamacare, the 2010 midterm elections, the 2011 collective bargaining fight, and the 2012 voting rights referendum. They engaged volunteers and identified supporters every day of it.

Instead of developing a robust list of supporters over the long haul, John Kerry in 2004 and Mitt Romney in 2012 treated Ohio's six million voters like a six-month project. Mitt Romney literally closed up shop after he narrowly won the 2012 Ohio Republican primary, then re-opened the same office for the general election. He would never catch up to President Obama's vaulted field organization in the state, which had numerous offices and staging locations and thousands of neighborhood team leaders in place before the Romney team even developed a field plan.

Ohio's Ready for Hillary supporters knew that we needed to start organizing because there isn't a day to waste in a battleground state like Ohio. If there is anything that activists can do today, to help win, they want to do it.

***

When the *Columbus Dispatch* and *Cleveland Plain Dealer* reported that I was joining Ready for Hillary, my phone was blowing up with calls and texts. One of my first calls was from former House Minority Leader Tracy Maxwell Heard. She asked, "what is Ready for Hillary doing in Ohio and how can I help?" Donors reached out on their own. Friends throughout the state were thrilled – not just thrilled for me, but thrilled to be able join the effort themselves. The outpouring of support from all corners of the state was tremendous.

The following dedicated Ohio Ready for Hillary superstars asked to be included in this book: Colleen Byers, Tracy Army, April Hammer, Sheena Kadi, Marquez Brown, Nick Tuell, Sara Valentine. Countless others were equally helpful but less demanding about personal credit!

***

In March 2014, I returned to Columbus for an Out & Ready for Hillary grassroots fundraising event orchestrated by Joel Diaz from our National LGBT Advisory Council and his now-husband (and my former roommate) Craig Scheidler. Ticket price: $20.16, of course. It was an incredible event attended by over 100 local LGBTQ supporters, including some older lesbian couples who had never stepped foot in Axis, the go-to dance club for shirtless male undergrads from The Ohio State University. State Senator Nina Turner spoke, along with Cincinnati City Councilman Chris Seelbach. Columbus's iconic drag queen Nina West performed, ripping off a black jacket mid-show to reveal her fabulous custom-made red sequin dress with a blue and white "Hillary 2016" across her chest, and later doing a photoshoot with Cardboard Hillary.

***

My Ready for Hillary colleagues moaned every time I started talking about Ohio. "If it were up to Seth, all of our money would go to Ohio," Alissa joked during our staff retreat.

Jill Alper, a Michigander who was running the retreat, gave a perfect reply: "Don't worry, Seth. It will happen eventually."

Yes. Yes, it will.

Part V: The Grassroots Tour

THE HILLARY BUS

"This is your craziest idea since the creation of this organization," I told Adam.

After class one day, Adam saw an RV dealer in Manassas, Virginia called "Reines RV." It was almost too perfect: buying an RV from a place called "Reines," because that also happens to be the surname of Hillary's longtime spokesman.

Trish Hoppey of the Pivot Group, consultants of ours since even before we could pay them, created the Bus wrap design and oversaw the installation process. Trish handled press advance for the Clinton Administration and organized a bus tour to promote then-First Lady Hillary Clinton's health care plan in 1993. Early on, Adam sat down with Trish for what he thought was a pitch for the Pivot Group to make money off of Ready for Hillary. He walked away with a $5,000 check from Trish instead. She believed in our cause from the beginning and it didn't even matter to her whether or not she was paid.

The Pivot Group designed a state-of-the-art wrap for the bus that even included a "Please Don't Text and Drive" public service announcement on the back with the iconic picture of Hillary wearing big sunglasses and checking her Blackberry.

On the sides, it said "Join the Movement" along with our logo and website, readyforhillary.com, in big letters. We considered a hashtag for the bus, but Nickie rightly pointed out that the one action we wanted people to take upon seeing the bus was to come to our website and sign up. Other features of the wrap design included: social media icons, a disclaimer and huge union bug on the back, and a "Powered by NGP VAN" on the front above the windshield.

We had an RV in mind that we wanted to check out. Eric called Reines to ask if we could test drive it. The response was "we only let people do that if they are serious about buying."

We not only bought the RV; we paid cash for it.

***

When Adam, Eric and I first saw the shiny, wrapped Bus for the first time, we nearly peed ourselves. It was everything we had imagined and more, and we couldn't wait to hit the road. Drew Xeron, a photographer based out of Washington, joined Trish at the shop of our wrapping vendor, Schneider Graphics in Des Moines, to take some professional shots so that we could show our Bus to the world. We then sought out some rural Iowa landscapes as backgrounds for photographs. Drew was quite a diva about the angles, the sun, the parking, the vantage point, and just about everything else. But it paid off, because the pictures were amazing. Before we hit the road, we posted a couple pictures on the Bus's new Twitter account, much to the delight of the Taj Magruders of the world. The Bus began tweeting about its journey in a first-person voice from its own Twitter handle.

***

"You cannot put a value on the brand you are trying to protect," one of our senior advisors relayed to us with regard to the Bus tour.

She was right.

The day before, the Drudge Report had proclaimed to the world that our bus broke down. That was inaccurate, of course, but it didn't matter. We had violated Craig's cardinal rule: "Do no harm." And it was my fault.

Even before we had the bus, we imagined potential problems, particularly with vandalism. I discussed this in depth with Alissa. As a communications guy, my worst fear was some crazy out there painting "BENGHAZI" in red paint across the side of the bus and TV cameras showing up to grab footage. The potential for vandalism to create local and national headlines was high, and this was a big reason why I felt the responsibility of being on the Bus.

Accidents were another obvious potential pitfall. Once I got behind the wheel, I began having recurring nightmares that the bus would drive off the road, off a cliff, off a bridge, injure a family, hit a kid on a bike, you name it. Even while driving, I had similar visions that ran through my head. An accident of any nature, while driving a bus with "Hillary" plastered all around it, would be a national spectacle. Just imagine if people had been hurt. "Hillary's Bus Injures Family" would be the headline. Her brand would be damaged. Right-wing nutjobs would be merciless. Even if someone else were at fault for the accident, it wouldn't matter. When it comes to anything that can damage Hillary on the Internets, facts aren't relevant.

***

The Bus wasn't always a joy ride. The close quarters – combined with the overwhelming responsibility of driving, executing stops, and doing our day jobs – made for some unhappy colleagues.

At the launch of our Grassroots Tour, Adam and I clashed constantly.

"We're not even out of the parking lot and you're already pissing me off," I told him as we made our first journey in the newly wrapped bus.

We butted heads over when to arrive, how often to stop, how long trips would take, and so on. Before too long though, Adam was comfortable enough with how the Bus tour was going that I took the reins and he went back to his day job at headquarters. Each time he tried to get back on the Bus I resisted. I love the guy, but he had better things to do, and the Bus was too small for both of our egos.

***

Being on the Bus meant navigating directions, deciding when and where to stop, addressing mechanical problems, staying on schedule, executing and event, sharing a hotel room, and doing it all over the next day. It was a challenge to begin with, but with me, it was impossible for some of my colleagues to handle.

While driving, I needed my co-pilot to check my email and texts, tweet for me, and respond to reporters as if it were me typing (while putting the commas in the right place and having proper line breaks!). Eric was trying to do all of this, while keeping up with his day job and being the contact for volunteers on the ground.

"I'M ON THE F***ING PHONE!" he screamed at me in our hotel room in Austin. The guy was going to have a nervous breakdown, and it was my fault. I immediately called Alissa and conferenced in Adam and we decided to send Eric home. He jumped up and down and gave me a huge hug when he found out the news.

***

In addition to spending quality time with colleagues, the Bus offered the opportunity to see friends and family across the country. My parents live just a few miles off the I-80/I-90 Ohio Turnpike, so I stopped at their house often.

When the wrapped Hillary Bus pulled into Woodville for the first time, the whole family was sitting on lawn chairs and waiting, including my grandmother who is approaching 90. My 9-year old niece Madi was wearing her "I Can Be President" t-shirt from Hillary's 2008 campaign. It still fit.

Emma was a realist about her twin sister's presidential aspirations, warning her, "You know it costs like three thousand dollars to try out…"

(Thankfully, Hillary has raised sufficient funds).

MISADVENTURES

"Getting there is half the fun." –English idiom

To be honest, I really don't know what we were thinking when we decided that our staff could drive a bus around the country. We had initially discussed hiring a professional driver, but that option was cost prohibitive. We went it alone. No one could have anticipated the mishaps we would encounter on the road, but we took it all in stride, fixed the problems and kept going.

***

I was the first to get behind the wheel, driving our brand new RV out of the Reines RV lot. There was a shopping center across the highway where we decided to practice driving. It took me five minutes to leave the RV lot, weary of any car in sight. We crossed the road as the RV bounced up and down. Eric screamed, "OH MY GOD!!" Adam was waiting in the shopping center parking lot, laughing and iPhone in hand. I turned in front of him, laughing. "DYING!" That was Tracy's reaction to the video Adam sent her. I missed every turn around the parking lot and had to constantly put the thing into reverse. The smaller vehicles in the lot were not amused. But ready or not, it was time to hit the road. We had no idea how to drive this thing, but at least it wasn't wrapped yet!

***

Tired and finishing up our first drive, Eric and I exited the Ohio Turnpike at Elmore, where I attended high school, to rest for the night at my parents' house in Woodville. I wasn't paying attention to help guide him, and WOW are those Ohio toll-booths narrow. He smacked the passenger side mirror into the pole opposite the toll booth, twisting the mirror inward. It left a mark, but we wiped it away the next day. We called Adam from my parents' landline to inform him of the bad news. At the time it seemed like a big deal; looking back, it was nothing.

***

Arriving in Iowa, we met up with Derek. He had arranged a parking location for our RV while we worked with Trish on preparations to have it wrapped. Appropriately, the location lacked an actual address and had only coordinates. No one would be able to find the location (including, initially, us). With Derek bravely leading the way, we drove back and forth around rural dirt roads in Central Iowa for a couple of hours. Murphy's Law then caused heavy rain. Finally, we found the undisclosed location, dropped off the RV and proceeded to get lost again – and stuck in the mud – coming back. We got out to push and nearly locked the keys in the door as it was running. Derek's car and the RV were caked with mud inside and out.

***

Eric hit a turtle. (I'm not kidding). The poor little guy flipped up into the air and spun, according to Adam, who was following the Bus and watching. Adam stopped to see how the turtle was doing, and was surprised to see him continuing to walk across the road into a field. Shockingly, he was only slightly cracked. A couple hundred meters after the turtle, a rabbit ran across the road and Eric had to slow down for it. It's unclear whether the tortoise or the hare won the race.

***

The first stop on Hillary's book tour was at Union Square in New York City. We arrived at around 2:00 AM that morning with no permit to park. After driving around and seeing some food trucks, Adam decided to drive over the curb and onto Union Square.

Since it was our first stop, we actually thought it was necessary to have three people stay and guard the Bus. Sean, Eric and I, who did the honors, called this task "Night's Watch," a Game of Thrones reference.

In the morning, a city worker knocked on the Bus door, asking if we had a permit. She was clearly a big Hillary supporter, conflicted between her support and her duty to clear the Square. "I love Hillary," she told us. "You're making my life very hard right now." She checked with her supervisor and eventually asked us to move.

We told her that our driver who had the keys was not there (my favorite delay tactic), and then I called Adam, who was catching a nap for a few hours at a nearby hotel, to find out what he wanted us to do.

Before Adam arrived, people started lining up in earnest for the book signing, and then things got worse as a particular profession of individuals approached.

"I think that's Liz Kreutz," Sean said, referring to the national ABC Clinton beat reporter.

All of a sudden, I had to entertain reporters who were seeing our shiny Bus for the first time, try to get in touch with Adam, and smooth things over with the city worker who was becoming more and more impatient. Helpless, I dramatically curled up into a fetal position. Eric laughed and took a picture.

One reporter, the *New York Daily News*'s Celeste Katz, was actually more interested in the Bus than in Hillary's book signing. Adam arrived shortly after Celeste, and I gave him the keys and began concentrating on the growing contingent of reporters congregating around the Bus. The scrum now included the mildly aggressive Japanese TV station NHK.

Adam, a law enforcement officer himself, always knew how to smooth things over on the spot. He negotiated with Secret Service and NYPD for a front-and-center spot off the actual cement of the Square. As he went to take the wheel, Celeste jumped on the bus. "Can I ride this thing?" she asked. SURE, what could possibly go wrong?

There were so many blind spots when driving the Bus, and it was impossible to see low objects from the high-up seats. As I heard the body of the Bus crunch, my heart pounded as a looked up at Adam and he gazed back with a similar "oh s***" bug-eyed look. He had hit a three-foot-high stanchion.

"Oh no!" the NHK reporter said a millisecond later.

"It's just a bump," I replied confidently. (It was definitely more than a bump).

Her cameraman headed over to get footage of the damage, and I ran in front of him to block his view. "Everything's fine," I told him, until he went away. I stayed there until we could get a chair to lean up against the bus to cover the damage.

In her very lighthearted story, Celeste passed off the incident as the Bus "doing battle with a stanchion."

We didn't successfully dodge that stanchion, but we did dodge a bullet. And later on down the road, my colleagues and I often mused about why it was a good thing that Adam was first to damage the Bus.

***

We arrived to the Chicago book tour event about 15 minutes after doors opened, missing an opportunity to sign up those who were at the front of the line. Under my breath, I blamed it on Adam's high number of smoke breaks.

While the Iowa Caucus was still more than a year-and-a-half away, we had a responsibility to sign up as many humans as humanly possible. Moreover, we needed to be sure that the FIRST people who entered were wearing Ready for Hillary stickers. That way, Hillary knew that we were organized and signing up everyone. She is an organizer by training after all. We came up short that day, but we made sure it never happened again.

***

There were six of us on the initial Bus manifest: Adam, Kirby, Eric, JoAnn, Sean and me. I insisted that Sean join us to help handle media, which was a good call. We compared it to the Real World, not just because of the close quarters, but because of the diversity of the group: The gay guy, the random young guy, the Asian guy, the black woman and the couple. Seating (and sleeping) arrangements were as follows: Adam driving, Eric co-piloting, Sean on the chair/stool, Kirby on the couch, JoAnne laying her head down on the kitchen table, and me in the bed, which became increasingly crowded with clipboards and signage.

We picked up another passenger on the way back from Chicago: my dog Mya. We now had an unofficial Bus mascot. Mya loved the Bus and even more so, she loved all of the attention she got from all of the people on and around the Bus. She was thrilled with all the random snack pieces that were on the floor and became quite the canine vacuum cleaner. Eric set up a cardboard "Mya barrier" around the driver seat to prevent her from bothering the driver.

Once while Adam was on the phone with Craig, Craig asked Adam to hold on for a moment, but Adam, still listening, overheard him say: "They have a DOG on that thing now! MAN... I don't control anything!"

***

We arrived in Philadelphia at about 4:00 AM. The rest of the team stayed at a hotel for a few hours, and I took a shower in one of their rooms before heading to the book tour event venue to park the Bus early.

When I arrived at the location I got about an hour of sleep before I heard people knocking on the door. They were volunteers who had arrived early. I told them to hang tight, but they had questions about the Bus and I had to accommodate them even though I looked and felt like hell.

Eric arrived soon after and took care of training the volunteers. He noticed that the steps to the Bus, which operated automatically when opening the door, would not extend because they were hitting the curb. He's a really smart guy and can always be counted on fix a tricky situation. So what did he do? He activated the hydraulics to raise the Bus just enough so that the steps would clear the curb and supporters would be able to get in and out safely and easily.

Meanwhile, I was emailing back and forth with Ben Terris, a Features reporter from the *Washington Post* who had asked to join the Bus for a leg of the journey. He had taken the Amtrak from Washington and was going to meet our staff and supporters, then ride with us back to Washington to get a feel of what being on the Bus was like. I hadn't really thought through what granting this type of access might mean – but it was going to be fine, right?

The event itself was great. We signed up nearly every person in line. Mission accomplished in this big battleground state, and it was a great display of support for a national reporter to see. But as we went to leave, something was very wrong. The hydraulics that Eric had lowered remained on the ground, refusing to raise. After multiple attempts, all of them raised except for the back passenger side. With the hydraulic's base on the ground, we would not be able to drive away even though the Bus was fully operational otherwise. We were stuck there until further notice. And the *Washington Post* was there watching it all play out.

Evan, who had driven up from Washington that morning, brought us a jack to attempt to raise the Bus enough to get under the hydraulic and force it up. Using a car jack to raise a monster 9 ton vehicle was not easy. It barely seemed to be raising even though we were turning and turning. Each rotation of the jack was more difficult than the previous, and Eric, Evan and I had to alternate as we wore ourselves out. It was a near useless endeavor, but we kept at it.

In between my turns at rotating the jack to lift 18,000 pounds, I tried to entertain our reporter friend. Adam, in disbelief, walked away and had a cigarette. I don't blame him.

Eventually we raised the Bus enough so that we could lodge a block under the hydraulic base. Then, by loosening the jack, the weight of the Bus coming down was enough to manually force up the hydraulic. But this only happened a little at a time. The entire process took about two hours, but I'll be damned if we didn't fix it ourselves and get on our way. Home free, I thought.

But all the while we were fixing the Bus, Twitter was ablaze with pictures and commentary about our mechanical mishap. It wasn't until everything had been fixed and we were on our way that I realized that the outside world had taken interest in what had just happened.

I was relaxing in the chair with Mya and chatting it up with Ben about how incredible it was that we just fixed the issue ourselves. Then, I started getting a string of frantic texts from Tracy. "What is going on???" After a few back and forth texts of me trying to explain, I went to the back of the Bus, in the bedroom actually, to call her and find out just how bad things were.

To me, we had fixed the problem and were back on our way. But to some observers across the country, Hillary Clinton's bus had a massive breakdown – DOOMING her potential candidacy.

Sure, the bus wasn't *actually* broken down, and Ben Terris never used those exact words, but it didn't matter. Perception is reality. Reading quickly through the right-wing celebration over the Internet about what was a minor issue we fixed ourselves, I realized that some haters across the country were cheering creepily for our failure, not just in politics but also in terms of safety.

We were independent from Hillary, but good or bad, what we did reflected on her. I should have known better than to invite a reporter to join us on the Bus. That was my biggest failure of my time at Ready for Hillary, and it was completely preventable.

Arriving back in Washington just as Hillary's event at The George Washington University was ending, we pulled out a few packets of posters to share with attendees as they trickled out.

As the event concluded, people began surrounding the Bus, smiling, taking pictures and grabbing posters. After word spread that we were giving out free posters, hundreds of people mobbed us. It felt as though people were lining up desperately for the last food on Earth. Eric and I rolled the posters furiously on the ground as supporters waited their turn. A Getty photographer witnessed the frenzy and captured the iconic moment. Eventually Eric and I just handed unrolled posters to each person until the very last person left the scene.

The day had gone from disaster to euphoria. Such were the ups and downs of this incredible journey.

***

Eric and I drove all the way from Harrisonburg, VA to Little Rock, AR in one day. It was a long drive, but we wanted to stay in Arkansas' capital for obvious reasons. The next day, at Alex's suggestion, we made a stop in "A place called Hope," where President Clinton was raised, and snapped some photos outside the former president's first boyhood home.

Later in the day we had a planned stop at Bexar County Democratic Party Headquarters in San Antonio, followed by a book signing event in Austin the next day. It was mid-June, so we had collected a massacre of bugs on the front windshield along our journey. We couldn't find the local Blue Beacon truck wash and didn't have time to get a wash anyway. So, I had Eric pull up all the way to a ledge and I stood atop that ledge, leaned over dangerously and used Clorox wipes to remove the bugs from the front of the Bus.

Yes, the job of Ready for Hillary Communications Director sometimes involved removing bug guts from the front of the Bus by hand. I can still smell them.

***

Parking was always the most difficult part. The responsibility of requesting a parking spot from a city or campus or other jurisdiction fell on my colleague Samantha Levison. Sam spent hours on the phone trying to secure the best spot possible, sometimes to no avail, and sometimes I wound up finding a better spot once I got there. Other times, I just drove around as Hillary fans dangerously thrust themselves toward my moving Bus to take pictures.

For one of the early book tour stops, we had a valid city permit with a clear time and location for our reserved spot, but local law enforcement wouldn't honor the permit for security reasons. We were annoyed at first, but thankfully, one officer on the scene had a brilliant solution: "Go park across the street and block those protesters."

Done.

***

Arriving at a hotel in Utah, I began to park. As I was maneuvering, Adam opened the door to try to guide me. But as he opened the door, the steps came out and hit the curb as the Bus was moving. The steps were stuck and would not retract. We had no way to fix this problem, as there was an entire motor system involved.

Adam drove for hours – with the steps hanging out – to find a mechanic, then spent several more hours helping him fix it. Rather than making sure we had working steps, the solution was to disable the system and revert the steps to the upright position and then lock them in place. It worked, although now we had to jump and climb to board the Bus.

***

The grueling, bumpy journey and a few sleepless nights on the Bus took a toll on my health. It was as if we were playing Oregon Trail, journeying west at a strenuous pace and putting the well-being of our travelers in jeopardy. "You have died of dysentery," BuzzFeed's Ruby Cramer told me, not being far from the truth. Eric was the first and I was the second casualty of the Westward journey. The Bus manifest had been reduced to just Kirby and Adam, as they departed Vegas without me and headed to San Diego and then San Francisco.

After two days straight of sleeping in my pet-friendly MGM Grand room, I was slated to fly back to Ohio with Mya and rest up more. But I missed my flight out of Vegas. Contemplating my options and realizing it was Pride weekend in San Francisco, I suddenly started feeling better and decided to head to the Bay Area and meet up with Adam and Kirby on the Bus.

***

The single instance of 'vandalism' occurred not in a Republican area but two blocks from Market Street in San Francisco's Castro district. The Bus was parked overnight and by morning, it had a graffiti-like orange symbol of sorts on its back passenger side. It was minor, and I contended that it was done by a supporter who thought the Bus needed a tattoo. We had planned to get that part of the bus re-wrapped, but Adam was able to remove the orange spray paint with Magic Eraser.

***

Ohio Turnpike toll booth, again.

This time, the mirror uprooted, coming off completely and hitting the ground. It happened so fast, we had no idea what had just occurred. Evan, my co-pilot at the time, jumped out to retrieve the mirror.

"Do you want to file a report?" a toll attendant came out and asked. Hell no, we didn't want to do that! I drove off, joking with Evan that I needed him to hold the mirror out the window so I could see.

***

On our second trip to the City of Brotherly Love, I had the great/horrible idea of taking the Bus to the famous cheesesteak joints, Pat's and Gino's.

Apple Maps, of course, took us through the narrow, brick streets for which the city is famous. I was doing alright driving until I approached an intersection with a road closure in front of me. The road we came to was a one way going left, but located on my left was a big USPS mail truck, leaving enough room for cars but not for the Bus. I couldn't go forward, right, or left, and I couldn't back up because there were an increasing number of honking cars behind me. I told Evan to get out and tell the people behind us to stop being so upset. Eventually, we decided to move some of the orange barrels so I could pull forward into the closed-off block ahead and at least let the cars behind pass while reassessing the situation. The construction workers ahead were thankfully nice enough help us navigate through their construction zone. Working people, saving the day again.

But then the real trouble came. Call it the hydraulics redux.

JoAnn was getting on the Bus – sans steps, since those hadn't been operating since Utah. As she got on, we suddenly saw blinding, white dust spraying all over the interior. After the dust cleared, we realized that it was in fact the fire extinguisher, which JoAnn had accidentally grabbed while boarding. Then, we realized we had an even bigger problem. It was as if the fire extinguisher had somehow triggered the hydraulics to go down. There's no other explanation. But once again, we were in Philadelphia, and once again, the same damn hydraulic got jammed.

JoAnn felt so horrible about the entire episode. Knowing that it would take a long while to fix, she loaded up a box of clipboards and signup sheets and went to the event location to meet volunteers.

The event was a Katy Perry concert – an absolutely perfect audience for us. Reporters were joking on Twitter about how there was no difference between a Katy Perry concert and a Ready for Hillary event.

Back at the Bus (which was thankfully parked at the back of a CVS and mostly hidden from public view), Evan worked on the hydraulic for about two hours, with limited success in forcing it up. He was pulling wood and other objects out of the CVS dumpster to aid in the process.

Finally, Neisha and I decided to go pick up a monster jack that could lift a gazillion pounds. We got the hydraulic fixed once again, and Evan got his workout for the day.

We then headed to the Wells Fargo Center, where Katy Perry's concert was taking place. Sam had diligently called the venue in advance and asked where we should park the Bus. But the lot workers started asking a lot of questions. After I politely protested, the lot supervisor came over and told me that political activity was not allowed in the parking lot. "It's really just a big bumper sticker," I tried to tell him.

We had to leave, and the trip was a bust.

***

I've said enough about the damn hydraulics. This time, though, I was on my own.

Rachel, Evan and I were wrapping up a Bus event at the University of South Carolina when we noticed we had the same hydraulics problem for a third time. Evan tried to help, but then he needed to leave to catch his flight. Rachel wanted to help as well, but she needed to drive to the College of Charleston for her first meeting with her campus team there.

So it was just me and the Bus. Knowing that it would take a while, I positioned the folded-up tables on the outside of the Bus so as to hide myself from public view. The ghost of Ben Terris still haunted me.

I worked on it for a while, trying to raise the Bus with the jack. But the crossbar in the back had been so badly damaged from our previous hydraulics repairs that the Bus was not raising one bit. I then pulled a Hail Mary, actually driving away and hoping the friction from the road would unjam the thing. The Bus's alarm was going off to let me know they hydraulics weren't all raised (gee, thanks), and sparks were flying all over the road. It wasn't working. I found an abandoned gravel lot to reassess the situation.

Then, I dug a hole directly under the hydraulic, so that I could fit the jack under it and force it up. It worked, and I was on my way to the College of Charleston, just in time to meet Rachel's very dedicated team and give them the opportunity to get their picture taken at the back of the Bus.

***

"Can you take the Bus to Salt Lake City?" That was what Alex texted me. I knew exactly why, and I knew I had no choice. But it was going to be tough. We were in Vegas and had an event in Denver the next day. Salt Lake City was not along the route by any means.

Utah was one of the "Craig states" – a name I gave the states he always seemed to talk about: Utah, Idaho, Minnesota, and Maine. All were early caucus states. They were important to Craig, and that was enough for me.

The day after the Vegas Pride parade, I drove more than 1,000 miles, because our Utah supporters wanted the Bus to come and I didn't want us to disappoint them. Craig had had a series of political meetings in the Beehive State the previous week. We couldn't tell our Salt Lake City supporters how important they were and then not bring the Bus their way.

After stopping in Salt Lake City, we made our way to Denver, arriving at Tracks, an LGBTQ bar in Denver, at about 11:30pm and signing up supporters for the next two hours. It was a long day that ended with Sean and me getting to our hotel at 2:00am. Early the next morning, we had planned for a stop at a park in Aurora. Waking tired and cranky, we hurried to get there.

We didn't have the right directions, and it was a big park. Jessica was already there but we didn't know exactly where to find her and we didn't have her number handy. Already late, we turned into what wound up being a dead-end tiny parking lot. The parking lot was completely full, with cars on one side and a ditch on the other. In other words, we could not turn around. We also could not back up easily onto the six-lane street.

I was determined to turn around anyway. Sean got out to help me nudge back and forth, doing what I commonly referred to as a "35-point turn." I inched back and forth a few times but ran out of room. Needing more space, I backed up a few inches off the pavement even as Sean told me not to. It would have worked, except the Bus would not go back up onto the pavement no matter how much I pushed on the accelerator and I couldn't back up to get momentum because then I would risk sliding down into the ditch. Getting more and more frustrated, I pushed the accelerator down to the floor to try to get back up on the pavement.

Then, all of a sudden, the Bus started jerking up and down uncontrollably, until eventually shutting off and immediately rolling down into the ditch before I had a chance to slam on the brakes.

Sean came running, asking me if I was okay. (To this day, I continue to reflect on how fortunate we are that Sean was not between the Bus and the ditch). I remained as calm as possible under the circumstances.

The Bus restarted, but the back end was lodged in the dirt.

The first thing I did was call Jess Mejia to tell her that we had trouble with the Bus and would need to cancel the event. I then assessed the damage. It was bad. But whatever damage there was, that was much less an immediate concern than what might happen if pictures of the accident emerged on social media. The park was full of people playing with their kids and watching a baseball game. A few small groups of people walked over to see what had happened.

"Everything's okay," I told them. "Everything's okay." In other words, stop staring and go away. Thankfully, they did.

As I called Jess, Sean looked up towing companies. "We will pay anything," I told him to relay to the person on the other end of the line. "Tell them it's an emergency."

It was. As a communications professional, I was well aware of the damage that I could do to myself, to Ready for Hillary, and to Hillary herself if pictures of this mess were posted on Twitter. The right-wing trolls would have a field day.

A tow truck was on its way and would arrive in 30 minutes. With more and more eyeballs looking over our way, I decided that we needed to cover up the Bus. Protect the brand, I thought to myself. Thankfully we had the foresight to invest in a tarp cover. It was beige and white, which would cause much less attention than what a big blue bus had been causing. Most importantly, it would prevent anyone from taking a photo with the word "Hillary" in it.

Sean and I began putting the tarp on, more quickly than we had ever done in the past, even though we had to navigate tree limbs now resting on top of the Bus.

Halfway done with putting up the tarp, a police officer approached. Ah f***, I thought.

"Hello sir. We want to cause as little disturbance to your community as possible," I said, without making eye contact so that he wouldn't engage in conversation. "A tow truck is on its way and we will be gone soon." Period, end of sentence. It was a godsend that he didn't take a report.

Once the Bus was covered, Sean and I turned our shirts inside out so we weren't walking around with "Ready for Hillary" on ourselves. A few other folks walked over to check out what had happened, but for the most part we were in the clear.

The next step, however, was going to be the hardest of all: I had to call Adam.

"This is a call I never wanted to have to make," I began, my voice shaking and him completely silent on the other end. "Let me begin by assuring you that everyone is alright. The Bus is stuck in a ditch. It's not great. Tow truck is on its way, I'm just trying to make sure no one takes a picture."

Adam was totally understanding and reassuring under the circumstances. "What's most important is that you are alright," he said. He told me he trusted me to make the right decisions about what to do next.

A few minutes later, the baseball game ended and many of the cars were leaving the parking lot. That was actually quite a blessing. With the cars in the way, there would be nowhere for the Bus to go even when a tow truck arrived. People stared a little as they moved their cars, but nothing like what they would have done without the tarp.

A few minutes later, the tow truck arrived. "We're going to do this as discretely as possible," I informed our tow truck driver, explaining what had happened. He made clear immediately that he was a big Hillary fan and he wanted to help.

We peeled back the cover just far enough to attach the chains. Before long, the Bus was dislodged from the ditch and pulled out.

Sean pulled out his wallet to give the truck driver a tip – $120 to be exact. It was a small, but sizeable portion of the money Sean won at the poker tables in Las Vegas.

We cancelled our events over the next two days, went early to Iowa, and found an RV mechanic shop outside Des Moines that got it fixed just in time to get rewrapped and be bright, shiny and new for the Harkin Steak Fry. No one would ever know.

So many things went wrong to get us into that situation: driving 1,000 miles the day before, lack of sleep, running late, not having directions and my irresponsibility behind the wheel. But so many things went right to get us out of that situation: the cover, the cars moving out of our way, the officer letting us be, the quick tow, the speedy repair job.

In the end, there were zero pictures, zero tweets and zero news articles from that day, and I could not be happier about it.

***

After a stop in Miami, Sam left early to scope out our parking spot while Taj Magruder (yes, Taj joined us on the Hillary Bus!) and I packed up the Bus. On my way out, I bumped into a parking meter, causing some mild damage to the wrap and reinjuring the back fiberglass in some of the same places as the Aurora incident.

Despite the mild damage, we needed to get to the book signing event right away.

After I parked, I was explaining to Sam what had happened as CNN's Dan Merica walked toward us. I stopped talking mid-sentence when I saw him.

"Well, if it isn't the Energizer Bunnies themselves," he said somewhat mockingly, invoking President Clinton's quote about Ready for Hillary supporters. But neither Dan nor anyone else saw the damage. We had strategically placed folded-up tables and palm branches (yes, palm branches) from a nearby tree in front of the damage. The only person on-site to notice was my buddy Brendan Corrigan, who was helping Hillary's advance staff. "Did you have an accident?" he asked.

"We don't use that word," I told him.

It was a hot day in Coral Gables, so I walked to nearest Publix and bought 500 bottles of water, catching an Uber for the three-block return trip. This was the final stop on Hillary's book tour.

After the event, Sam, Taj and I had some "arts & crafts time" back at the hotel, putting duct tape and an array of spare wrap on the Bus to make it look good as new.

***

Taj and I left Florida and headed to Philadelphia for Hillary's first 2014 campaign rally. Somewhere in North Carolina, I noticed flashing lights in my rearview mirror. Sheriff's deputies were pulling me over. I wasn't speeding, was I?

One of the deputies asked me to follow him outside, taking me to the back of the Bus, pointing to one of my tires and saying, "your tire there smoked a little bit when you changed lanes." I responded, "I'm sorry officer..." He then interrupted me, "Really we just wanted to be sure you weren't texting and driving," an obvious reference to the message on the back of the Bus.

They never asked for my name or driver's license. They were apparently just bored.

***

A group of students from Boise High School saw on social media that our Bus was going to be at Boise State, so they walked over on their lunch break to grab a poster. Realizing they were going to be late getting back to class, I offered them a ride in the Bus. They were ecstatic. "Nothing like this ever happens in Boise," they told me.

As they directed me back to their school, they texted their friends, saying that the Hillary Bus was coming to Boise High. We arrived at the school to a small group of students who had apparently left class to come see the Bus. Then, teachers were bringing their entire classes out to join in. I hadn't meant to cause so much commotion.

"Hey Seth, you might want to leave," one of the students told me as he witnessed the school principal on his way over. I left right away.

***

Already low on gas, I made three quick drop-offs at three universities in San Francisco, leaving Kendall at one, Ian at another and a Bay Area volunteer, Julie Soo, at a third. San Francisco didn't have many gas stations and certainly not many that would fit the Bus. I located a station on my phone and was in route, but it was too late. I ran out of gas.

Immediately, I called Sean and told him to monitor social media for anyone tweeting about the status of the Bus. It was on an entrance ramp, front and center. I put on the flashers and the emergency brake. It was getting dark. I then called emergency roadside assistance and waited forever, waving off traffic and rerouting folks to a different entrance ramp so that fewer people would see the Bus.

Six law enforcement vehicles drove by and must have thought nothing of it. You know, a big blue bus with Hillary's face on the back, blocking an entrance ramp… nothing to see here. Twelve tow trucks passed as well, but none was sent to help me. Two hours went by.

Desperate, I called Ian and told him to have his friend take him to a gas station. He arrived with a 2-gallon jug of gas, which should have been good for at least a handful of miles. But the Bus still wouldn't start.

Two-and-a-half hours after my initial call, roadside assistance arrived and put 10 gallons in. The Bus started, and we were on our way, never taking the same chance again.

***

Near a university somewhere in the Southwest, I found myself in a dead-end construction site at the edge of campus and needed to turn around without much wiggle room. Three workers at once began trying to help me back out.

After a few attempts and a lot of "help," I seemed to have found a way to exit. One of the guys motioned to me indicating that I had cleared everything, and they all waved goodbye. As I pulled out in front of the guys, I heard a noise coming from the back.

"Did we hit a Porta Potty?"

"Unclear. Do those guys look mad about it?"

"No, they look confused."

"Alright, let's go." And we drove away.

HAPPY TRAILS

Crossed the deserts bare, man
I've breathed the mountain air, man
Travel, I've had my share, man
I've been everywhere. –Johnny Cash

Despite the magnitude of the responsibility and some tense moments, the travels were mostly carefree: driving along, logging miles, taking in the scenery, snapping photos, stopping to eat and get gas, unloading, holding an event, reloading, resting for the night and starting it all over the next day. 45 states. 60 college campuses. Hundreds of events. 40,000 miles.

We were inspired by the support for Hillary in every corner of the country. There were honks, thumbs up, smiles, even screams of joy. There were also more than a few middle fingers – every single one those from a man. I responded to shows of support and disdain in the same way: by honking appreciatively, waving and smiling. When a hater emerged in the lane next to me, I was reminded of Hillary's incredible line in a 2008 primary debate:

"Well that hurts my feelings."

***

Having free reign of the Bus meant that I got to make a whole lot of friends happy.

We stayed overnight in Savannah, Georgia so that David W Moore – who I only knew from his enthusiastic Facebook posts – could see it.

Sergio de Leon, a prominent Hillary supporter in Tarrant County, Texas, implored me to bring the Bus to his neck of the woods, and he organized an amazing event at the Cowtown Diner in Fort Worth, complete with a mariachi band.

Our South Florida journey included a stop to see Craig and Wayd on Sea Turtle Lane.

Former Albuquerque mayor Marty Chavez quickly organized a Hillary Bus house party at the home of supporter Ethan Epstein, where U.S.

Senator Martin Heinrich and Congresswoman Michelle Lujan Grisham made appearances.

I made house calls with the Bus back home in Columbus, weaving through narrow Clintonville streets so that Craig and Joel could get a photo in their pajamas, then heading over to Bexley to see Elisabeth Hire and Chris Hayler along with their parents, newborn, and dog.

And no visit to Chicago would have been complete without swinging by Tracy's condo and driving her aimlessly around the city.

***

And now, please enjoy some of the best quotes from our time on the road:

"Is she in there?" –everyone

"Is she running?" –nearly everyone

"So she's running, right?" –insistent ones

"Why would you have a bus if she isn't running?" –a fair question

"Who pays for this?"

"Do you sleep in here?"

"Hillary Clinton is out there!" –guy in a gas station

"Hillary Duff?" –cab driver in Detroit, seriously

"I know what Ready for Hillary is. What is a Ready for Hillary bus?" – woman on NJ Turnpike

"Are you guys the Ready for Hillary from Facebook?" –young couple in Oklahoma

"This bus is not Ready for Hillary." –passerby in Philadelphia, as we were fixing the hydraulics

"You changed my mind! I no longer like Hillary!" –a dose of sarcasm from me to a detractor

"I know she's sleeping. But I want you to tell her about my economic plan..." –thoughtful fella

"...I'm not voting for her. But if she implements my plan, I'll vote for her the second time around." –ibid

"We're losing votes!" –when we inadvertently angered other drivers

"Did you get a special license?" –most people

"Get out of this state." –truck driver

"You know what? We like it here. We think we'll stay a little longer." –Adam, in response

"This is grassroots at its finest." –college student in New Mexico

"I'm taking this picture of your bus for my wife." –polite older guy, clarifying

"It's okay if you like the bus." –me, assuring straight dudes that their love for Hillary didn't need to be projected onto their moms and girlfriends

"Atthehillarybus" –NH state senator, in an actual tweet, apparently trying to tag the bus

"What difference, at this point, does it make?" –our motto when things weren't going well

"I'm the driver!!!" –Eric, to Adam and me, loudly and on multiple occasions, reminding us that he was behind the wheel.

"God dammit, Sam!" –me and other Bus riders, whenever any logistics got screwed up, including ones that had nothing to do with Sam

JOIN T –the side of the bus when you opened the door, instead of "JOIN THE" with the door closed

"You probably want to close that door so people don't take pictures when it says J-O-I-N-T. There's a lot of pot smokers in Fayetteville." –helpful woman and tour guide

"Ouch." –Evan's caption for a never-posted @thehillarybus tweet with a pic of the side mirror detached

"Does it take the bus longer to get places than a car?" –a colleague, seriously

"This is my favorite photo EVER." –Millennials, about the "Texts from Hillary" photo on our posters

"This is probably the worst photo of her I have ever seen." –a Baby Boomer, about the same photo

"It's free. It's a poster. It's a legitimately free poster. And if you would like THIS poster I'm holding in my hand, you're in the right place at the right time because we're giving them away for FREE! But, actually. That's why people keep walking away with them. 'Why are you giving away these posters?' Because we love Hillary Clinton! 'Free posters?!? Oh my gosh I love free posters,' said everyone always. 'What a fantastic [insert day] surprise. Kendall, that's so nice of you.' Oh, no problem, [insert name of university], I do what I can." –Kendall, yelling out on every college campus

"Even buses powered by millions of supporters need gas." –my explanation to environmental activists

"YOU drive this thing?" –reasonably concerned friends

"Seth drives Hillary around!" –my grandma, despite multiple attempts to correct her

"This is the best thing that's ever happened in Woodville!!!" –a neighbor, when I visited my parents

"That thing goes all over the road. It looks dangerous." –a concerned mother who also happens to be a prominent reporter

***

It was an absolute privilege to be behind the wheel of a vehicle that captured the hopes and dreams of the millions of Americans who wanted Hillary to run for president. It was quite possibly the most important thing I have ever done.

An amazing adventure through 45 states. A Bus with Hillary's picture, seen by hundreds of thousands. Many smiled, many waved, many took pictures and many took posters. But now the wrap has come off, and now my watch is ended. (And now my watch is ended).

Part VI: Reflections

WHO MATTERS

At the end of summer 2014, a Washington-based media outlet had eight Washington insiders provide an "analysis" of Hillary's book tour. These contributors were political experts, no doubt, but not a single one of them had attended an actual event on Hillary's book tour. Missing from these analyses, of course, was any mention of the multitude of supporters who came out to meet Hillary everywhere she went. How was it that thousands of everyday Americans from all corners of the country participated in Hillary's book tour, but no one in Washington seemed to notice?

It was our job to remind the world of who matters.

Here's my analysis of the events I attended: Thousands of enthusiastic supporters stood in line for two hours or more to get their five seconds to say hello to Hillary Clinton. The crowds represented every fabric of this great country. Moms pushed their mothers in wheelchairs, fathers held their impatient daughters' hands, LGBTQ couples had their arms around one another, and people of every race, religion and creed filled the lines waiting for their chance to see this woman they so admire.

***

In Seekonk, Rhode Island, an eight-year old girl named Tara approached Hillary wearing an oversized "Hillary for President" shirt that came down to her ankles. Later on, a local news station asked the girl what she said to Hillary. Her response: "I told her, 'I'm ready. Are you?'"

Millions of Americans were Ready for Hillary before Hillary was ready, and they are the inspiration for this book. Here are just a very few of their stories:

<u>Taj from Pennsylvania</u>

Our fundraising consultants suggested having two young grassroots volunteers speak at the Ready for Hillary National Finance Council Meeting on November 2013 in New York City. Adam and I joked that the grassroots volunteers' portion of the presentation would come off like a scene in the Hunger Games. In reality, it was a brilliant idea and would serve as a symbol of what this movement was all about.

We selected Taj Magruder and Haley Adams as our two volunteers. I called Taj – it was actually during his birthday dinner – to let him know, and he was elated. Haley, a Students for Hillary team leader at Yale University, was equally excited, and her appearance at the finance council meeting parlayed into a future appearance on Up with Steve Kornacki, during which she touted Hillary's support among millennials.

Meanwhile, in Washington world, I was loading up the *New York Times* with information for a curtain-raiser piece on the Finance Council Meeting. At David Brock's suggestion, I gave the *Times* new insight into our list-building enterprise and offered up many prominent supporters for interviews.

We had worked for weeks on that story and a lot was riding on it; all of the finance council members would be reading it the very morning of the meeting. "No getting away from this," I thought, "this is New York and this is the *New York Times*." Failure was not an option.

As the story came out, I was grabbing a late dinner with Taj nearby our hotel. "Oh my God, you're in here," I yelled out, informing Taj that his name was in the story and trying to lighten my mood as my heart sunk while pouring over every sentence. As I rushed through the story, I glanced quickly across the table. Although he was trying to hide it, Taj was crying. I pretended not to notice so as to not embarrass him.

It was so easy to get wrapped up in the insider drama, as if nothing in the world mattered other than what our big donors thought about one story. After all, they were going to glance at the story proudly but briefly (I bought copies and placed them all around the room). Yet merely the mention of his name in a Hillary-related *New York Times* piece changed the world of a kid making around $30,000 a year, with friends and family calling, texting, and writing on his Facebook wall all night long. His reaction that weekend was even more significant than the collective reactions of the generous donors I had worked so hard to impress.

***

Daniel from New York

Daniel Aubry's life, as indicated in his Twitter bio, is a "sassy mix of Hillary Clinton and Mrs. Fields." He latched on to Ready for Hillary early and was one of the many supporters I had the opportunity to meet thanks to social media. The 2008 campaign had nothing like this – the ability to connect with supporters online and harness their excitement. This is what Daniel represented to our movement. He wasn't one to attend a house party or a fundraiser, but he could sure be counted on to call out right-wingers over criticism of Hillary and show his pride for our movement by, for instance, making Hillary-themed goodies at his bakery.

After a year of Twitter exchanges, I met Daniel at Hillary's book signing event at Union Square in Manhattan. He just had his book signed by Hillary and he was beaming when he showed it to me. I was disappointed that he didn't bring me anything from his bakery, as I had been requesting.

He did, however, wear his red "HOT for Hillary" shirt so that Hillary could know how much he loves her. We snapped a photo together in front of the Bus and I tweeted it. Trolls came out of the woodworks with their gay-bashing comments, courtesy of a Daily Caller article that embedded my tweet. Daniel laughed it off.

Over the months that followed, Daniel would go in and out of touch. I later heard from Taj – he and Daniel had become buds on Twitter over their shared love for Hillary – that Daniel had leukemia and was undergoing multiple rounds of chemotherapy. It sent shockwaves throughout our headquarters when news came that *both* Daniel and Taj, two of our biggest supporters and each of them being under 25, had contracted cancer. We sent them each Ready for Hillary pillows signed by the entire staff.

Adam called me when I was in South Carolina on the Bus tour to tell me his plans for the Harkin Steak Fry, specifically which supporters we would fly in. "Make sure you include Taj and Daniel Aubry," he told me. "I don't think Daniel will come, but he will appreciate being invited," I replied.

I texted Daniel immediately and asked if he had any plans the weekend of September 14. The gist of his reaction was: 'I'm in chemo. I can't do anything.' But when I told him we wanted to fly him to the Steak Fry to join fellow Hillary supporters, his tune changed quickly and he promised to talk to his doctors as soon as possible on Monday morning. The doctors were able to give him a break from his care and he came to Iowa with us.

A few months later, he took to his sassy Twitter account to let the world know he was in remission. (Taj is fine too!)

***

Martha from Florida

Avery and I took off from Washington for North Charleston, South Carolina. The famous Blue Jamboree was being held the next day, featuring Jennifer Granholm. Ready for Hillary secured her as the speaker at the request of our friends in the South Carolina Democratic Party, so naturally we sent the Bus down for the occasion

The night before the event, as we went to check in at our hotel in North Charleston, we were ambushed by another guest at the front desk. She interrupted the check in process, nearly yelling.

"OH MY GOSH! Are you with the Bus? Can I get a t-shirt like yours?"

For a moment I regretted having worn my identifying shirt inside the hotel. Her enthusiasm was borderline embarrassing, both for us and for her Republican friends that she was traveling with. "I'm just trying to check in, lady," I thought.

But then she started telling her story.

She had emigrated from Guatemala with her family at the age of 7 and lived in the United States for the past 35 years. At no point did she seriously consider going through the process of becoming an American citizen until Hillary ran for president in 2008.

"I didn't get my citizenship in time to vote for her last time, but now I am a citizen and it's because she inspired me," she told me. "I live in Florida and I will vote for her there. She is my hero."

Avery then ran out to the Bus to get her some free stuff, and she continued to tell me her story.

"I lost my job yesterday," she told me, "but knowing that you guys are out there, doing what you do for Hillary really makes me happy."

Knowing there were supporters like Martha made it worth doing.

***

Andrew from Indiana

In early summer of 2013, Adam checked the P.O. Box and found quite a surprise: a three-dollar, cash contribution. The cash was accompanied by a note from the contributor who explained that he didn't have a credit card but that he would vote for the first time in 2016 and wanted his first vote to be for Hillary.

His name was Andrew Hoffman, a 14-year old from Evansville, Indiana. Adam wasn't sure that we could legally take a contribution from such a young donor. He emailed Jim, attaching a picture of the kid's note.

(Congress, in the McCain-Feingold bill, had prohibited federal political contributions from individuals under 18 years of age, a provision later tossed out by the Supreme Court. Hell, if they're going to let the Koch Brothers pour in a billion dollars, the least they could do is let this guy give us three!)

Later, when we sought to reach out to him to highlight him in a grassroots supporter spotlight, we didn't have an email address or phone number for him, so we used the same snail mail address on the envelope he sent us and asked him to send us an email. He emailed us a few days later, humbly stating, "Hi. I am the person you wrote a letter to."

When the Ready for Hillary store was launched, he again sent us cash in the mail, requesting his items, paying the exact amount to the penny, and explaining that he did not have a credit card. We moved his request to the top of the pile.

***

Erin from Oregon

I didn't know anything about her, but the enthusiasm of her 140ish-character tweet gave me enough confidence change our schedule and add hours of driving time to our Western adventure.

Ready for Hillary's staff knew that if we made just one supporter's day, we had done our job. We were a full block away from the parking spot Erin secured for us at the University of Oregon, and already she and her friends were jumping up and down in the street, directing me as if I were a pilot who had just landed at the Eugene Airport.

I told her that I could give her just one hour before we needed to hit the road for our California stops the next day. Through some social pressure among UofO's sororities, she delivered 113 sign-ups in a single hour on a Sunday. After we wrapped up, we took a few extra minutes to give Erin a ride back to her sorority house. She was giddy about the whole day.

***

Marty from Illinois

Some guy named Marty Malone from Chicago took Twitter one day, bashing Ready for Hillary's social media graphics. He was a Hillary fan but thought that Ready for Hillary's images were embarrassing. Rather than dismissing him or being insulted by him, we asked him to make graphics for us.

He had expected to be ignored, but instead he was asked to play a role and to put his skills to use. We'd send graphic requests his way and he would turn them around quickly and for free. It was the perfect example of empowering a grassroots supporter, and a story that Adam told constantly.

***

Jack from Arkansas

"Seth, how do I get on this bus?" That was a question from a kid who wanted to join me on the tour, after he got my cell phone number through sheer persistence.

"We really need you in Arkansas, Jack!" He understood my response, and kept his head down and did what I had asked. Jack loved Mike Ross and Mark Pryor, and he was as devastated as President Clinton when they both lost.

I hope someday soon he is able to retire from his job at McDonald's and follow his love of politics. I think he has a promising career ahead of him.

***

Renay from Michigan

Ready for Hillary was Renay's "me time." Her husband would jokingly nag her about how much time her love for Hillary was consuming in her life.

She retweeted just about everything from us – but always in the evening because she was a school counselor. She admired Hillary so much, and saw her as a role model for her two girls.

I met Renay at one of the first Ready for Hillary events – back when we had black rally signs because they were printed wrong and we didn't have the money to have them reprinted. She drove her daughters two hours from Detroit to Grand Rapids, where Hillary was speaking to the Economic Club.

When we decided to take the Hillary Bus to Netroots Nation in Detroit, Renay was the first person I told. She met Sean and Evan at our Bus event earlier that day outside the "Fishbones" restaurant in Greektown, which was owned by a prominent Clinton supporter.

I expected her to just drop by, but she grabbed a clipboard for herself and one for each of her daughters to sign up supporters.

"I raised them well," she bragged.

When I invited her to the Ready for Hillary/Rising Tide Interactive "Motown" After Party, it was one of those invitations you give just to be nice and you know the person will immediately decline. Not Renay. She came and she stayed until we closed down.

After she arrived, I pulled Nickie over and introduced her and Renay. She thought I was merely introducing her to a friend, but then I told her "Renay's the one on Twitter with the two girls," she realized that Renay was one of our prominent social media supporters.

"OH MY GOSH! It's so good to meet you. Thank you for all of your support," Nickie said. "I love meeting our Twitter supporters in real life." A long conversation followed.

She wasn't there officially with Ready for Hillary, she didn't attend the Netroots event, and she was a few years older than most other attendees – anyone else would have felt out of place. Renay fit right in.

The next time the Hillary Bus Grassroots Tour came to Michigan, Renay of course was there. She was one of the first people in line when Hillary came to Oakwood to campaign for Michigan Democrats.

I began to introduce her to Quentin, who was joining me for this particular leg of the Bus tour, but of course she already knew him, having attended his Black Americans event in Detroit a year prior.

After the event, she took us to dinner. As we left the parking lot, Quentin said to me, "She doesn't even want anything from us. She just wants to be part of this. It's amazing."

***

Shelly and Jo from Washington, DC

Shelly and Jo asked for – and promptly received – business cards to legitimize their role as Ready for Hillary National Finance Council Co-Chairs and help them raise money to fulfill their $25,000 commitment.

They were besties who found themselves on opposite sides of the 2008 primary between then-Sens. Obama and Clinton but even so, they remained close.

They were key early validators for Ready for Hillary when it was just catching on. It was a perfect example of two supporters who were eager to help and just needing a little bit of support themselves.

***

Marc and friends from Nebraska

He didn't love Hillary nearly as much as he loved pizza. But he loved Hillary enough to give $3 for the chance to get free pizza.

Our digital team held a contest in which any supporter who made a $3 contribution was automatically entered to win a pizza party on the Hillary Bus.

132

Marc, a student at Creighton University in Omaha, Nebraska, was the winner of the contest. So we scheduled a time to take the Hillary Bus to Omaha in August, on our way from Colorado to the Harkin Steak Fry. But when I crashed the bus in Aurora, we of course had to postpone the Omaha stop. Poor Marc wondered if his free pizza would ever come.

After the Steak Fry and following our tour of Iowa colleges, my colleague Gracie and I backtracked a bit west to Omaha, getting a much-needed oil change when we arrived. "I've never seen darker oil come out of a vehicle," the mechanic told me. "She had better win!"

Marc's order included a cream cheese pizza and other delectable creations from a specialty pizza locale. Sean worked with him to get the order just right.

We expected it to be super awkward: Pulling into a pitch-black community next to a park and feeding children pizza. It had a sort of "creepy ice cream truck man" feel to it. But Marc's friends were awesome, spending most of the time making fun of their good friend and claiming to be the only Democrats in Nebraska. I gave him a hard time about only making the minimum suggested $3 donation, but he had won his cream cheese pizza nonetheless.

***

Phyllis from Kansas

The University of Kansas was an amazing stop, even though the ink in the pens froze solid. Needing a break, I made my way to a residential area to lay down for a while.

Finally finding a spot, started catching up on some emails. But moments later someone knocked on the door. Having just laid down, I was annoyed and I considered not answering.

When I answered, I met an older woman who was so excited about the Bus. Nothing new. But it wasn't her excitement she wanted to tell me about. She told me about her friend who was in the very late stages of M.S. and might not make it much longer.

"She caucused for Hillary in 2008. She hasn't had much good news lately, but this will make her day," the woman told me as I handed her two bumper stickers.

I forgot the name of the woman who came to the door, but I will never forget the name of her friend, Phyllis. I hope Phyllis has the chance to caucus for Hillary once again.

"Thank you for answering the door," she said, keen on my initial hesitation to do so.

"No, ma'am, thank you for knocking."

***

Dick from Minnesota

A World War II veteran in his mid-80s, Dick stopped by Hillary's book tour stop in Minnesota wearing his military cap. Dick didn't have a ticket to get his book signed, but he wanted to come to the event and stop by the Hillary Bus to show his support. I will never forget his proud, smiling face as he showed us his Ready for Hillary Founding Member Certificate, signed by Adam. He received the certificate for being one of our first supporters. He volunteered at the table for a while, then he walked home, certificate in hand.

***

Anonymous

Sean and I were outside an LGBTQ bar (of course) and had two sign up tables. The tables were busy and I was helping a few guys sign up while telling them about Ready for Hillary and encouraging them to vote in November.

Out of the corner of my eye, I saw a taxi driver slam on his breaks, run over to our table, sign up on a clipboard, and take two bumper stickers. Before I could say hello, or even thank you, he was back in his cab driving away. The entire process took less than 30 seconds.

*

One of our first events was in Naples, Florida, while Hillary was giving a speech across town. The media extensively covered our event: 4 cameras including Univision, 2 daily newspapers, and radio.

We had advertised the event to local Democratic groups, with Avery making the calls and successfully building a crowd. But the enthusiasm for Hillary shown that hot day was not limited to Democratic activists. Two women, tellers at a nearby bank, saw us rallying and ran, literally ran, out of the bank during their lunch hour, borrowed signs and joined the rally. I made sure every media outlet knew!

*

"How's your day going? Will it be better when we move our bus?" Kendall could always be counted on to tell it like it is. This is how she addressed two women in parking enforcement uniforms at the University of Colorado – Boulder. I was taking pictures of the large crowd of students surrounding our sign up table and overheard the conversation.

"Just pull up to the curb over there. We'll let you stay."

It was a huge relief to me – the streets were full of snow and ice, as could be expected in Boulder for that time of year. It was my first experience driving the Hillary Bus in snow. Their generosity in bending the rules just a bit was a random and beautiful act of kindness. These two had one request, though.

"It's going to cost you a poster." Best. Trade. Ever.

***

The nurses, the line workers, the waitresses, the small business owners, the farmers, the teachers, the miners, the truckers, the soldiers, the veterans, the students, the hard-working men and women who support Hillary Clinton don't always make the headlines, but they will indeed help write America's story if she becomes President of the United States.

READY TO END

As Ready for Hillary's end neared, we had the important tasks of preserving our resources, cleaning out the office, and wrapping up loose ends.

We made it abundantly clear to our supporters and to the media that if and when Hillary decided to run for president, Ready for Hillary would wind down its operation. Especially as Hillary's decision neared, it was vital that we provide clarity about our end game to everyone both inside and outside of the Ready for Hillary movement. The media's grand interest in a potential Hillary campaign gave us ample opportunity to deliver that clarity. If and when Hillary stepped in, we would be ready to step aside and make our list of supporters available to the campaign.

Weeks before Hillary's announcement, we exchanged our supporter list with EMILY's List to make sure none of the hard work of our supporters was lost and to make sure that this list was ultimately available to the campaign. Our friends at EMILY's List also inherited Ready for Hillary's millions-strong social media platforms to integrate into their Madam President project.

The Hillary Bus was set to be bequeathed to EMILY's List as well. That was the plan at least. In truth, the Bus never spent a day in EMILY's List's possession, because we decided to sell it in order to pay off bills. "I know you are DEVASTATED," I sarcastically told Jess McIntosh from EMILY's List. I don't think anyone over there wanted that Bus anyhow, and I don't blame them.

After driving and sometimes living in it for the better part of a year, I cleaned out the Bus – a task that took more than three hours. Pens, clipboards, placards, snacks, phone chargers, toiletries, make-up, you name it. The Bus even had an overflowing "Lost & Found" section of clothes left behind by the 20 or so colleagues who joined the tour at one point or another. Whoever removed the Bus's wrapping found a good deal of duct tape on the back bumper from various arts & crafts times. There was scattered damage to the fiberglass, something that Craig pointed out to me months later at Adam's wedding.

Letting go of the Bus was like saying goodbye to a friend who I spent months and months taking care of. As difficult and stressful as it often was, many days I wish I were still on I-70, I-40, I-80 or I-95, waving at fans and taking in scenes of this beautiful country that so few people really get to see.

***

We had closeout sale after closeout sale for the Ready for Hillary Store. 40 percent off this, 50 percent off that... we were practically giving stuff away. In fact, we ultimately donated the clothing to a women's homeless shelter. My colleagues worked day and night to help Connor and Iran fill thousands of orders that came in toward the end.

Sam orchestrated the sale of furniture, appliances, TVs and just about everything else to clear out our office and have a little money to pay some of our final bills. I scored a microwave and a desk. The staff closed out the headquarters in late April, just days after Hillary had declared her candidacy. Iran removed the Ready for Hillary PAC sign from the door and Nickie sent around a picture of the moment along with a beautiful note thanking everyone for their efforts. When I visited Adam in Brooklyn in May, I rented a U-Haul to bring to him the last of his furniture from the office. The rest of the space was completely empty. Sean and Evan helped me load up the furniture, and our headquarters was no more.

In compliance with Federal Election Commission regulations, Ready for Hillary PAC became Ready PAC on the day Hillary announced. (Independent groups can't include the name of an official candidate). The Hillary Bus, again just a plain-old RV, was sold for $46,000. Not bad. The new owner has no idea of the stories that Bus could tell.

***

Looking back, it's worth thinking for just a moment about what the political world might have looked like were it not for the existence of the Ready for Hillary.

Everyday Hillary supporters would have been demoralized that Washington insiders told them to sit on the sidelines. All of the media speculation in 2013 and 2014 would have focused on Hillary herself, rather than the hopes and dreams of millions of Americans who wanted her to run. She would have wrongly been seen as an establishment-only choice rather than someone with enthusiastic grassroots support in every corner of the country.

Hillary's grassroots army would have taken much longer to build. Prominent supporters would have needed to be wooed rather than immediately put to work. Her volunteer lists would have been sorely outdated. The Democratic primary field might even have been a little different.

But for the encouragement of millions of grassroots supporters, Hillary may have never run at all.

***

The millions of Americans who joined the Ready for Hillary movement will never know the full extent of the impact they had on the 2016 election. They will never know the full extent of the impact they had on the now-candidate herself. But they should know with absolute certainty that they moved Hillary Clinton a giant step closer to becoming President of the United States.

***

There are way too many people to thank.

Everyone who signed up, posted, tweeted, Liked, Shared, displayed a bumper sticker, raised, tabled, clipboarded, hosted a house party, hung up a free poster, and organized social networks... you made this possible. This was YOUR movement.

The 135,000 Americans who owned a piece of the Ready for Hillary movement, particularly the members of our National Finance Council and Millennial Council and the hosts and organizers of our events.

My colleagues, particularly Adam Parkhomenko and Sean England. Our interns, fellows and volunteers. Craig, Tracy, all of our senior advisors and many others who advised us behind the scenes. The Iowans, Granite Staters, South Carolinians and Nevadans who stepped up and helped build the Ready for Hillary movement in their states. The countless local, state and national public officials who leant their support. The 2014 campaigns and Democratic state Parties.

Rising Tide Interactive. The Pivot Group. 270 Strategies. NGP VAN. Catalyst. The Bonner Group. Windward Strategies. KKPromotions. Julie Wertz Design. Frank Chi and company. Rags of Honor. Facebook.

David Brock and everyone working for him, especially our friends at Correct the Record.

Priorities USA.

EMILY'S List.

The American workers who proudly assembled, printed and shipped the products we sold in the Ready for Hillary Store. The men and women of the U.S. Postal Service, and all of our brothers and sisters in Labor.

Anyone who's ever been counted out but refused to be knocked out.

Anyone who led, followed or got out of the way.

The press corps.

All who made the Hillary Bus Grassroots Tour possible: the Americans who designed and built the Hillary Bus, Reines, Ace RV, Camping World, Schneider Graphics, the construction workers, the Blue Beacon truck washers, the well workers, the refinery workers, the gas station workers, the mechanics, the toll plaza workers, the parking officials, local law enforcement, the college administrators, the students, College Democrats, the Students for Hillary teams, the fast-food workers, the cooks, the servers, the food delivery drivers, the bartenders, the front desk clerks, the housekeepers, the janitors, the everyday Americans who helped us park, and every person who stopped by, waved, honked, or gave a thumbs up along the way.

Friends and family who encouraged me to write this book.

The entire State of Ohio.

The dedicated staffers and volunteers in Brooklyn and around the country who are working to make history. The millions of Americans who want her to be our next president and are working to make it so.

Last but not least, Hillary Clinton.

***

Nothing like Ready for Hillary had ever been done before, and nothing exactly like Ready for Hillary will ever be done again. The combination of grassroots hunger and organizing necessity along with a potential candidate of such high caliber made the Ready for Hillary movement a once-in-a-lifetime success.

Hillary may never know about the adventures across the country of a Bus with her name and face on it. She won't get to meet all of her supporters who joined this movement. She may never know exactly how much Americans wanted her to run for president. And who knows… she may never even become president. There's no telling what the future may or may not hold.

No matter what, I hope she knows that people across America believe in her. They are inspired by her, her leadership, her life, her voice, her values, and her record. They wanted so badly for her to run for president, and they want so badly for her to be president. They will be with her every single day of the Democratic primary and if she is our Party's nominee, they will be with her until November 8, 2016, when we could shatter that highest, hardest glass ceiling once and for all.

It's not going to be easy. Breaking barriers and making history never is.

But if Hillary Clinton becomes President of the United States, America will have a champion for women, children, and middle class families. The most powerful person in the world will for the first time be a woman. A young woman named Chelsea whose grandmother was born before women could vote will hold the Bible as her mother is inaugurated as president. The world will celebrate. Bill will become First Gentleman. And the woman who sits behind the desk in the Oval Office will build on President Obama's record of helping the middle class. She'll work to raise wages and get government working for the American people.

America is indeed Ready for Hillary, and fathers are Ready to whisper in their daughters' ears, "See? You can be anything you want to be, even President of the United States."

140

Part VII: Memories

Supporter Adam Smith models a long-sleeve tee made by Rags of Honor, a print shop that employs homeless veterans.

Frenzy ensues on the eve of Hillary's big announcement. MSNBC's Alex Seitz-Wald (near left) checks his iPhone to monitor latest developments.

Ready for Hillary staff, interns, and volunteers pose for a picture the day before the 2014 Harkin Steak Fry in Indianola, Iowa.

Off-roading somewhere in the Southwest.

JR's Bar in Washington, DC gets decked out to celebrate on the day
Hillary officially announces her candidacy.

The Hillary Bus visits Miami Beach, Florida.

One of more than 100 house parties on our Day of Action. Supporters of all walks of life joined the Ready for Hillary movement.

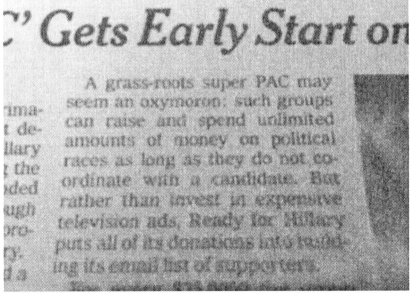

" *Gets Early Start on*

A grass-roots super PAC may seem an oxymoron: such groups can raise and spend unlimited amounts of money on political races as long as they do not coordinate with a candidate. But rather than invest in expensive television ads, Ready for Hillary puts all of its donations into building its email list of supporters.

The *New York Times* published a major piece on Ready for Hillary on the day of our first National Finance Council meeting.

Tracy and Mitch Stewart of 270 Strategies appear on MSNBC to discuss
efforts to organize grassroots Hillary supporters.

Marc and friends from Omaha, Nebraska take a break from their pizza
party to pose with Cardboard Hillary on the Hillary Bus.

Kate Maeder interviews with a local television station in San Francisco as fellow supporters rally behind her.

Jessica Grounds poses with supporters following a Women for Hillary grassroots organizing meeting.

Former Michigan governor Jennifer Granholm joins South Carolina
Democrats at the Blue Jamboree in North Charleston.

The Hillary Bus visits Sanford Stadium in Athens, Georgia. The
University of Georgia was one of many campus stops on the tour.

Cardboard Hillary meets Herky the Hawk at the University of Iowa.

Iowa students show their support for Hillary and commit to vote in the
2014 elections.

Eric takes matters into his own hands at Drake University, standing atop his rental pickup truck and using a bullhorn to attract students.

Texas supporters hold a house party to show their support for Hillary.

10,000 Iowans pack the Balloon Fields to see Hillary at the 36th Annual Harkin Steak Fry.

The Hillary Bus visits the Utah State Capitol.

At Orlando Pride, "Out & Ready for Hillary" supporters use a rainbow-colored picture frame to show their support for Hillary.

En route from Las Vegas to Reno.

The Sousaphone section of the Wolf Pack Marching Band stops by the Hillary Bus at the University of Nevada, Reno.

REDD-E.

College of Charleston Students for Hillary team leaders grab a quick photo with Rachel following an organizing meeting.

The final Harkin Steak Fry was an opportunity to honor the legacy of Tom Harkin and support Iowa Democrats in 2014.

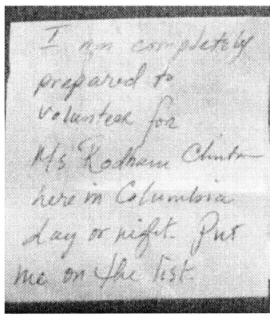

A supporter in South Carolina left this incredible note on the windshield of the Hillary Bus.

Students at Penn State University in State College, Pennsylvania grab clipboards and sign up with Ready for Hillary.

Tulsa, Oklahoma supporters join their former mayor, Kathy Taylor, for a
Ready for Hillary parking lot party.

Students and faculty of The George Washington University line up for
free posters following Hillary's speech.

Hendrix College students in Conway, Arkansas are Ready for Hillary, even before classes started!

Someday, Little Rock may need to clarify which "President Clinton" they mean. Sheila Bronfman and the Arkansas Travelers are ready!

Supporters join U.S. Senator Mark Warner and Congressman Bobby Scott for a $20.16 grassroots fundraising event in Richmond, Virginia.

The Hillary Bus visits the Pennsylvania State Capitol.

Ready for Hillary celebrated reaching one million Facebook supporters.

"Charlie the Butcher" poses in front of his famous restaurant in Williamsville, New York. A picture of Hillary, marking her visit to the restaurant, is on the wall.

The Hillary Bus, naked.

The Hillary Bus visits Sweetness 7 Café in Buffalo, New York.

The Hillary Bus crosses the Piscataqua River from Maine to Portsmouth, New Hampshire.

Dick Raatz, a proud veteran and proud Hillary supporter, shows off his Ready for Hillary Founding Member certificate.

Evan (left) and Sean (right) don't look too thrilled during the Hillary Bus venture to Niagara Falls.

The Hillary Bus visits Hillary and President Clinton's first home – now a museum – in Fayetteville, Arkansas. They were married in the living room, where Hillary's wedding dress is on display.

Blue Beacon Truck Wash workers get the Hillary Bus bright and shiny.

Children in Austin, Texas wave to the camera after getting their books
signed by Hillary.

Huge turnout at a Latinas for Hillary house party.

A young guy in Kansas City, Missouri does his best Hillary impression.

A kitty peeks out of a Ready for Hillary canvassing bag.

Nickie speaks about digital strategy to attendees at Netroots Nation in Detroit, Michigan.

The Golden Gate Bridge.

Sara talks about Ready for Hillary with supporters in Cambridge,
Massachusetts as they wait in line at Hillary's book signing event.

The Hillary Bus arrives at 2:00AM at Union Square in New York City for Hillary's first book signing event.

Karl Rove gets something right.

Pulling up to the Grand Canyon.

Photoshoot in Detroit, Michigan. The itinerary was mapped out by longtime Clintonite Jill Alper.

Dayton Mayor Nan Whaley joins Miami Valley volunteers at The Greene in Beavercreek, Ohio.

This little pooch is Ready for Hillary!

Kids take a break from the pool to pose with a Ready for Hillary placard.

Cleaning the bugs off the windshield...

A Place Called Hope: Bill Clinton's first boyhood home.

Sometimes, Hillary-themed goodies magically showed up at Ready for Hillary headquarters.

Mya sits patiently as I roll posters inside the Hillary Bus.

Congresswoman Sheila Jackson Lee of Texas poses with supporters.

A clean interior of the Hillary Bus. (photo credit: Liz Kreutz)

Ready for Hillary Senior Advisor Craig T. Smith chats with Iowa Democrats at Exile Brewing Company in Des Moines.

My pieces Emma (left) and Madi (right) and I during a break at my parents' house in Woodville, Ohio. (photo credit: April Hammer)

More than 600 supporters packed into Ready for Hillary's $20.16 grassroots fundraising event in Chicago, Illinois, joined by U.S. Senator Dick Durbin, Congresswoman Jan Schakowsky, and other supporters in Hillary's old stomping grounds. (photo credit: Tracy Sefl)

A Grand Rapids, Michigan television station goes live at the top of the hour from a local Ready for Hillary event.

U.S. Senator Tim Kaine of Virginia announces his support for Hillary at a South Carolina Democratic Women's Council breakfast in Columbia.

Ready!

One of several models of our Ready for Hillary onesies.

Mother Jones produced some amazing art to accompany reporter Patrick Caldwell's profile of Ready for Hillary's cofounders.

Our pet supplies were a big hit. Designer Julie Wertz was always full of great product ideas and marketing strategies.

Ready for Hillary staff and interns gather up to watch a special CNN segment about our organization.

Ready for Hillary Store products included magnets, shirts, lanyards, highlighters, coffee mugs and iPhone cases. All proudly made in the USA.

Supporter Corey Bailey holds up a placard in Naples, Florida as cars honk for Hillary.

State Senator Molly Kelly (near right) is introduced at a full house party in Keene, New Hampshire hosted by activist JoAnn Fenton.

Lisa addresses a crowd of 300 supporters at a $20.16 grassroots
fundraising event at Town Danceboutique in Washington, DC organized
by local activist Lane Hudson.

Kendall signs up students and passes out free posters at the University of
North Carolina at Chapel Hill.

Ready for Hillary mobilized supporters for the 2014 midterm elections.

Lol.

The initial order of "Bubbles Glasses" sold out within two hours.

It was a cold and windy day in Nashua, but Sean Downey had things under control.

While running Ready for Hillary, Adam was also a full-time undergraduate student at George Mason University. In 2003, he put school on hold to work for Hillary. She told him it was important to finish.

Shades? Check. Smartphones? Check. Badass Hillary look? Check.

The Hillary Bus traveled more than 40,000 miles and visited 45 states.

Expecting chaos after Hillary's event in Louisville, Kentucky, we set out many stacks of posters and allowed supporters to grab their own.

Boise High students got a ride back to school on the Hillary Bus.

Ready for Hillary's Pittsburgh supporters sent this huge banner to Hillary.

The Hillary Bus visits THE Ohio State University in Columbus, Ohio.

Students at the University of Kansas grabbed free Hillary posters between classes on a cold December day

I gave Election Day rides to the polls at the University of New Hampshire in Durham. With solid numbers there, both U.S. Senator Jeanne Shaheen and Gov. Maggie Hassan won their hard-fought re-election campaigns.

For 328 University of Colorado Boulder students, free Hillary posters went great with the snow.

Gnarlz and Jonathan encourage students to vote.

The Students for Hillary team at Saint Anselm College made the trip to Nashua, New Hampshire for Hillary's final campaign event of the 2014 midterm elections.

Students at the University of Wisconsin-Madison signed up in droves.

Me: Something looks off.
Adam: What are you talking about? It's perfect.

Ready for Hillary staffers gather with Ron Schneider (second from left) and his wife Beth Cooper (fourth from left), at the Steak Fry. Ron helped Adam get Ready for Hillary on its feet early on.

It took a few tries, but Abby got it right.

One of Adam's best early Facebook creations.

Parking wasn't always this easy, but at the University of South Carolina in Columbia, we had a great spot.

No one was better engaging supporters than Allida.

The Hillary Bus visits the Massachusetts State House in Boston.

Well-deserved.

Following a shirtless race, fraternity brothers at the University of Rhode Island sign up to support Hillary and now-Governor Gina Raimondo.

Parked between semi-trucks in Utah.

The original four: (L to R) Judy Beck, Allida, Kirby, and Adam, at Hillary's book signing event at Costco in Arlington, Virginia. For Judy and Kirby, Ready for Hillary was always a family affair.

I forgot to eat a pastry on air during my first appearance on MSNBC's Up with Steve Kornacki. This was Steve's first show, in April 2013, just days after Ready for Hillary's official launch.

Ready for Hillary Allida (far right) and Senior Advisor Ann Lewis (second from right) with supporters at a reception in Bethesda, Maryland.

The Hillary Bus sits in front of a beautiful Oregon landscape.

Ready for Hillary staff photo. (front row, L to R) Kirby (Hoag) Parkhomenko, Amy Wills Gray, (second row, L to R) Neisha Blandin, Quentin James, Alissa Ko, Rachel Schneider, Gabi Kahn, Alex Smith, (third row, L to R) Jessica Grounds, Lisa Changadveja, Jessica Mejia, Amy Drummond, Evan Wessel, Nickie Titus, Eric Jeng, (fourth row, L to R) Joanne Antoine, Seth Bringman, Craig T. Smith, Christopher Guerrero, Sean Downey, Kareem Absolu, Derek Eadon, Adam Parkhomenko, (fifth row, L to R) China Dickerson, Hans Goff.

Spectacular view of St. Louis skyline from across the Mississippi River.

The first photo of the wrapped Hillary Bus took Twitter by storm. (Photo credit: Drew Xeron)

Adam rented this billboard on Fleur Drive in Des Moines, next to the airport so that national reporters could see it during their travels.